PERSISTENCE,ATTITUDE, MOTIVATION CAN GET WHAT YOU WANT

BECOME VERY PERSISTENT AND SUPER SUCCESSFUL

I0840963

Gautam Sharma

(Dedicated to valued readers)

COPYRIGHT

Copyright 2018 Gautam Sharma all rights reserved, including right of reproduction in part or in full in any form. Copying or distribution in any form prohibited.

Table of Contents

1. Introduction

2.Persistence- a mindset & ability

3. Why does persistence matter?

4.Ways to become persistent, motivated

5. Beingeffective personally& professionally

About the Author

 Other Books by the Author

INTRODUCTION Can you guess what common attribute has made many men and women extremely successful and renowned over centuries and across continents?From Alexander the Great(356 BC) to Cleopatra, Genghis Khan, Michael Angelo, Joan of Arc, Mahatma Gandhi,Winston Churchill, Marie Curie, Einstein, Thomas Edison, Benjamin Franklin to present day outstanding people as Bill Gates , Warren Buffet , some other billionaires and world leaders. Its not just mental or physical prowess,talents, education,training or good fortune. The outstanding common attribute among all accomplished people of excellence across all space and time has been the quality of persistence, attitude and motivation.
It's about keeping on going towards their goals in the face of denials, obstacles, failures and opposition. The unstoppable keep on going, whatever the odds, slowdowns or roadblocks and they achieve success , victory and fame. This book will help explain the magic of persistence, motivation and determined attitude. If there is any single,proven formula to get most

things that you want in life, it is persistence .
Let us look at what it is and why it is so
important ? Persistence is the attitude and
the personality trait to continue with
determination on a set course of action to
overcome difficulties,failures or opposition
until the required goals are achieved.
These are several reasons why persistence is
important :

1. It shows that you are ambitious and that
   you have high goals and objectives to
   achieve. In as much as cause and effect
   Since you want to go places, you will
   have reason to find ways to reach there.

2. Your ambition and subsequent drive make
   you stand out, make others notice your
   determined,dominant personality.

3. Persistence makes you garner skills,
   experiences and abilities. The process of
   working harder to overcome failure
   helps you acquire new, peripheral skills
   or hone onto the basic,current,ones.

Working harder helps build inner strength
   and stamina. The determination to think
   and work is to keep going on doing
   activities methodically and consistently
   going step by step doing activities that

are required for your goals. Reasons
Why Persistence is the Key to Success?

In simple words, persistence means the attitude and personality trait of working hard and trying again and again until complete success is achieved. Here is why persistence is the key to success and why you should develop it as a vital personality trait.

1. Persistence makes you an expert

You may not be good at doing something for the first time but you will get better at it when you keep trying for the second time, third time and so on. With persistence, you will continue to do the same thing over and over again until you achieve complete success. This will make you an expert in whatever task you are doing.2. Being persistent will motivate you to try harder. Being persistent means that you will keep trying again and again. With every attempt, you will inch closer to success. It will motivate you to put more effort to get closer to your goals when you see that there is an actual difference between where you stand right now, and your previous effort. Self-motivation is an important aspect of being successful.

3. Persistence is a sign of being ambitious

Only those people who are highly ambitious can incorporate persistence into each and every little thing that they do in their daily lives. When you keep attempting something with persistence, everyone around you will look at you as an ambitious person. It will build a positive personality image for you, a key in shaping the outlook of a successful persona.

4. Persistence will set a good example to your associates and peers.

A reason why persistence is the key to success especially in workplaces is because your colleagues and subordinates will be inspired by your level of persistence. When they see you achieving your goals with determined persistence, they too will try to imitate this trait. This will result in an overall boost in productivity and efficiency for your team, making persistence a highly regarded personality trait at any workplace.

5. Persistence teaches you the value of success

Are you under the false notion that success can be achieved easily by manipulative tactics? Do you think that success can be easily bought? Do you think that success comes with just a little bit of effort? If have these untrue thoughts in your head, persistence will teach you that success is not that easy to achieve. As you keep attempting to achieve a goal over and over again, you will understand the true value of success. It will enlighten you about the amount of hard work and dedication required to make something happen, preparing you to give your best shot at everything in life if you want to be successful.

6. Persistence will help you gain experience

Being persistent means getting up after a failure, learning from your mistakes and trying again. This whole process will help you gain experience, which is vital if you want all-rounded success. Multiple number of attempts at the same thing will help you find out the things that can go wrong, the things that are crucial to a process or the things that are not required at all. This experience, which was a result of persistence, will teach you stuff that books and procedure manuals don't.

7. Persistence will make you aware of your weakness

To be successful, you need to be aware of your weaknesses and your faults. Your weaknesses will only be exposed when you analyze your failures and try to find out the things you lack to accomplish something. This is only possible if you are mentally prepared to accept failure, try again, fail again and keep trying until you iron out all your weaknesses to finally succeed. This is why being persistent is the key to success. Two most words for a lifetime of achievement , success, fun , happiness , joy and fulfillment: "Keep going. Keep going towards the light, your goals , towards the promise of so much goodness that awaits you. With joyous feelings, hope in your heart , and a song on your lips, keep going and receiving achievements , success , love, friendships, fame, fortunes and all else you had imagined. See the pure white light beckoning you, find your path through whatever comes in the way and keep going.

Persistence-The State of Mind

Success is something we all wish for, isn't it? Undeniably, those who attain great things are those who don't know when to give up. Whether you wish to achieve something or want to lose a few pounds or any goal that you are willing to succeed in, you need to be strong and persistent. Indeed the most successful people in the world have the key quality of perseverance which makes them assume impossible actions to be possible. How many of you can claim with confidence that you have applied persistence and consistency in your everyday life with some measure of success? I think the majority of us dream of incredible things but just lack persistence or the willpower, to follow through to accomplishment. People give up too soon as they have the wrong expectations of themselves and the results. They expect the mode to be easy, and they are amazed when they find the reality to be contradictory. Their enthusiasm quickly melts and they quit. What does being willpower and persistent mean? It is a cliche to simply say "don't give up".

One of the best illustrations persistence is the state of mind and sustained effort necessary to induce faith. In other word it exemplifies that determination mixed with Persistence backed by the desire makes a strong tool to ensure the achievement of the goals". The meaning of the term persistence is the quality that allows an individual to continue doing things even if it is tricky or opposed by other people. This is not something someone does with external goals; however, it is something someone does internally. Perhaps we all are aware of the fact that in the face of pain, anguish, suffering, and defeat; it is not easy to stay persistent. In simple words, persistence means the personality and attitude trait of working harder and harder and trying again and again until success is achieved. Abraham Lincoln is a leading example of persistence and strong willpower in action. Known as one of the renowned presidents in history, Abraham lost 8 elections before he, in the end, became president. He also lost his fortune when he starts losing his business twice and could have chalked himself up to being a loser, but he didn't. However, he didn't lack his determination and believed he could achieve his dreams. If you are passionate about something, chances are you're determined in moving toward it. It is the quality that allows the person doing things even though it is difficult or opposed by other people.

WCHAPTER One

What is persistence and why does it matter?

The conventional definition of persistence is: "not letting go or refusing to give up; persevering persistently; firm or obstinate continuation in a course of action in spite of trouble or opposition." It is a developed state of mind much like grit. It is the trademark of achievements since persistent persons push through difficulty, anguish, and pain which refers to the setbacks and roadblocks when pursuing an objective. As the significant component of self-discipline, determination and persistence also provide its own inspiration and motivation. You become more enthusiastic to do something incredibly when your activities started showing results. For instance, when you want to lose all those extra pounds and start exercise and to workout, you will be more enthused when you lost 20-25 lbs and your present wardrobe starts fitting loose Persistence can conquer almost any challenge. When you turn your mind to something and are eager to do everything it takes, including patience, willpower putting in the time and adjusting your plan to get there, you will eventually know the supremacy and power of determination. Some of the major factors or symptoms of lack of persistence are indecision, not being clear in what you want, lack of proper planning, weak desire, fear of criticism, feeling of insignificance and lack of going all out. You may not be fine at doing something for the first time but you will get better and better at it when you keep trying and believe in yourself for the second time, third time and so on. With persistence and consistency, you will continue to do the similar thing over and over again until you accomplish complete success. This will make you a proficient in whatever job you are doing. You have to believe that your victory is guaranteed and no obstacle will stand your way.

Billionaires and political leaders had failed several times and have thought of giving up college but they finally come out ahead as big winners. Edison also made more than 10 thousand experiments before he accomplishes something in making the first talking machine. As the primary factor of self-discipline, persistence also provides its own motivation. You become enthusiastic to do something when your actions started showing great performance and results. Courageous persistence is the main factor than any other that can promise success. And success is somewhat we all want, isn't it? But to be victorious takes persistence. Whether you want to lose your extra fat, get an A in a class, or any goal that you want to succeed in, you need to be persistent. It is the difference between a successful result and a failed one due to giving up.

Perseverance has other names — determination, persistence, a can-do attitude. When getting starting on your vision for success, first and foremost you need to identify your desires and wants. It is when you know the why; you can get a source for inspiration and keep yourself encouraged next, figure out how to achieve what you want? This makes it easier to attain it. Make your objectives actionable every day and follow through. All your objective-setting and planning will go to waste if you won't be able to build up discipline and good habits. Be positive in your work that you will attain what you want. Perseverance separates the losers from the winners. Those who persevere understand that luck is something only failures believe in. Success in life depends on your motivation to never give up, even when the reward is delayed.

How to stay persistent?

Like all states of mind, persistence is based upon specific causes. Take a piece of paper and write down a life goal, what you desire, and answer the questions; what is your definite purpose. Knowing what one longing for is the former and, perhaps, the most important step toward the growth of persistence. Strong motive forces can easily overcome many hurdles of our life. Similar questions like why do you want to accomplish this goal? How will it profit you and the more essential, how will it benefit others? In order to survive your purpose, you have to keep the focus on why you want this purpose/ goal or what the positive results will be in your life? We do have to keep in our mind that our purpose in this world is also to add value to others. If your wishes focus on your own gratification you will sooner or later fail or die a lonely miserable life.

All successful people who have attained great things in their life did so through both willpower and persistence. Even when they failed, they got encouragement and kept going. But we all know that staying determined and persistent is difficult. In any conversation of the qualities of the most successful people, it is always declared that Persistence is one of the, most significant factors in success. Major success rarely comes easily or without an enormous deal of attempt. Often the only distinction between those who succeed and those who do not is the capacity to keep going long after the break has dropped out. It is comparatively easy to persist when things are going smoothly and we see progress, however, great persistent people have found several means to keep going in spite of major setbacks and a lack of confirmation that they are driving near toward their goals.

Some of the significant things that persistent people have in common that keep them moving on long after so many people have given up:

Visualization for success

Persistent people have a vision or goal in mind that encourages and drives them. They are often visionaries and dreamers who see their lives as having a high purpose than simply just spending their life. Their vision is deeply entrenched, and they concentrate on it continuously and with great energy and the state of mind. They often think of this dream first thing when they wake up and the last thing prior to they go to bed. Accomplishing this goal becomes the crucial and focal point of their life and they dedicate a major portion of their time and energies towards attaining it.

- **Unshakeable self-confidence, self-belief**

Those persons who defeat the hurdles and accomplish greatly are often illustrated as "marching to the beat of their own drummer." Persistence people know what they wish for and are seldom swayed by the view of the masses. To have the perfect intelligence of who they really are, allows the persistent to carry on without being seriously affected by what others think of them or, being appreciated, or being understood by those around them. At the same time as that inner confidence gets shaken, but never gets shattered and continuously acts as a source of courage and strength.

- **A Inherent passion to succeed**

There are so many inspiring Entrepreneur and motivational who always speak, "If you really desire to do something, you will surely discover a way. If you do not, you will find an excuse." Persistent people never look for any excuse. What keeps persistent people going is their potent level of desire. Repeated failures, losing periods and dead ends, when it seems like no progress is being made, often come before some breakthroughs happen. Persistent people with high will-power have the intensity, state of mind, and inner energy to keep them motivated and going through these hard-hitting times.

- **Talent to Adjust and Acclimatize**

Persistent people have the capacity to acclimatize and adapt their action plan. They do not stubbornly persevere in the face of indication that their plan is not running but look for enhanced ways that will increase their probability of success. The motivated and persistent see their life journey as a bunch of dead ends, adjustments, and deviations, but have total faith they will reach their final objective. They are not attached to their ego and are rapidly willing to admit when something is not working. In addition, they are fast to adopt the fresh ideas of others that have been shown to work well.

- **Key success habits**

    As someone truly said, "Motivation is what gets you going ahead. Habit is what keeps you going."Highly - persistent people know it is very tricky to stay constantly motivated, chiefly during hard and the most difficult times and when it appears that no development is being made. They have come to rely upon their self-developing and discipline habits they can count on to carry on the path toward their ultimate goals. They believe the results of the hard work they make today may not be seen for a longer time, but they strongly believe that every single thing they do will count toward their end results.

- **Commit ment for learning new skills**

Persistent people understand the worth of any objective and reaching will take attempt, time, and constantly learning new skills and thoughts patterns. They welcome fresh ideas and change and continue searching for means they can incorporate these into their lives. Ongoing learning is seen as part of a continuous process through which the highly persistent continually expand the range of tools that they have to work with. Naturally curious type persons not only see learning as a way to reach their objectives more quickly, but they also see self-learning as a way of life. Learning and constant growth do not end at a certain age or phase of life, but they are the spirit of life itself, and thus never-ending.

- **Role models as mentors, motivators**

While it may come into sight that highly persistent people act without help and don't require any person, most have carefully chosen peoples they follow and admire. These can be individuals who are truly involved in their lives as guides or they can be figures who they have read about and who have extremely impacted them. Such people are often misunderstood on the grounds that they can make those around them feel uncomfortable. The ingrained models assist motivated persons to maintain and motivate themselves in an atmosphere that is not always kind and supportive.

The winners' circle defines persistence as refusing to give up when faced with opposition or hardship. It could be expressed as simply as trying again and again until you keep scoring at sports, maintaining relationships or succeeding at work or businesses. The greatness that you have, the greatness of the condition, is not calculated by what is accomplished. It is calculated exactly by how many times you pick yourself up and try to accomplish something. Among all of the values and morals we can have, it seems persistence is the consistent element in most people who thrive and succeed, no matter what they are succeeding at. We all seem to understand or know that all popular personalities have persistence in huge quantities. They have to keep their mind strong, keeping the boundaries of patience in order to attain the new records. Yet, you can see persistence all over the place you look, even for the job you get paid to do, so there ought to be something incredible to it. If in case you are evaluating what amount of struggle it would take to give your career a boost up, you might come across in the direction of your own persistence. You need to be clear about what you are determined to achieve. What is the result you are in the hunt for? If you need to gather knowledge or resources, then go get them. Once you have your objective, your plan, and the resources, then goes after it with dedication and enthusiasm. Stay focused every day until you get the outcomes you defined. It is also OK to occasionally get propped up by close relatives, family or friends to keep the required attitude that comes with persistence. Persistence is not about the trouble-free road, even though few people make attaining success look easy. Persistence is about systematic and continued to do something even when there is the good reason to give up. Persistence is about the basic confidence of knowing your vision is the right thing to pursue.

Make persistence a lifelong habit

Another most significant piece to having the higher persistence level is having support. Sometimes when it came to the list of things we wanted to accomplish personally, having a team of people who were above or on your level made you want to persevere and keep going for your aspirations. It is healthy and nice to have a supportive team like family, close friends, relatives, religion and particularly mentors that can be there beside you when you necessitate an additional boost up of motivation. Support from others is always advantageous, but not always simple to find. If you feel like you don't have a mentor or guide in your support team that you could, in fact, talk and sit down to about your aspirations, make an effort to find one, particularly one that has been where you are and who is at present where you are aspiring to go. There is no sense in having a support team that cannot bond and connect to your goals for the reason that they do not have any aspiring goals themselves. You need to evaluate your crowd cautiously and warily. Having a good imagination and thoughts also helps when it comes to persistence. When you can visualize and think about your "dream future" no matter what that might be, these visions every so often can get you through the harsh days. Do not let one failure in your journey of life to success dictate your motivation for the rest of the life. Each and every step is to bring you closer to your ideas and dreams, and when you can clearly notice your upcoming "dream future," you can fully fashion it under your own conditions.

Persistence in the provision of an ultimate crucial goal calls out numerous other virtues in you. You will push yourself to further than what is comfortable to achieve your chosen goal. Furthermore, you should know why you desire your goal in the first place. Plus, your why must be bigger than the difficulties and complications. The bigger the why the better the outcomes, Persistent people have a transparent goal or vision in mind that inspires and induces them. Reaching this ultimate goal becomes the central focal point of their life journey and they devote a larger percentage of their time toward reaching it. If we would like to succeed, we have to pay the price. And the way to success is long with a lot of hurdles and obstacles. No wonder most of the people stop at one point or another after running into the obstacle or barriers. Only the handful of people has this special quality to keep moving forward, and these are some people who succeed. Persistence is essential. Persistence is probably one of the most worthy and excellent characters a person can possess. It's the ability to be determined to accomplish something regardless of any obstructions and setbacks. Hence, arm yourself with the right state of mind and the right tactics to overcome failure. Perseverance or Persistence is mainly about the basic optimism of knowing your dream is the right thing to chase. In fact, there is no other way to succeed and achieve something huge but by developing persistence in your life, and here we would also share a few significant ways to develop it.

Do you believe in persistence?

Aren't you? Persistence is being able to continue an human action until one has succeeded, like winning a race. When you start running, you keep on pushing yourself until you have crossed the finish line. Or instance, in special education, having persistence in teaching a kid until he/she has reached their ultimate goal is like a race. You are persistent in helping them reach their destination and don't stop until they have reached their objective. People tend to hold on to their beliefs even when it seems that they should not. Persistence is the tendency to cling to one's initial belief even after receiving fresh information that dis-confirms or contradicts or the basis of that belief. Every single person has tried to change somebody's belief, only to have them obdurately remain unchanged. For example, you may have had such debates concerning the abortion, or evolution.

In the plethora of cases, resistance to challenges to belies is defensible and logical. For instance, if you have always done well in racing, getting the third position on some race should not lead you to abandon your belief that you are generally good in the race. However, in the handful of cases, people cling to beliefs that logically should be abandoned, or at least altered. There is overpowering evidence that smoking increases the probability of contracting cancer and that exposure to media violence heightens the likelihood of aggressive behavior. Even, some people strongly deny these scientific facts. People expend considerable mental energy to maintain their opinion when presented with facts that prove them wrong. They will concentrate on experiences that support their point of view merely will ignore any experiences, even their own, that give grounds that they are wrong. They will do the same thing with any other kinds of evidence as well.

Types of Belief of Perseverance

There are three types of belief perseverance exist —1) social impressions 2)self-impressions, and 3) social theories. The first kind of belief consists of beliefs about the self, considering what one believes about his skills and abilities, including body image and social skills. The second type comprises one belief about specific others, for instance, a parent or best friend. The third type comprises mainly what one believes about how the world mainly works, comprising how people act, feel, interact and think. Social theory opinion can be either directly or indirectly learned which means that they can learn through experience as a member or they can be taught. In the first case, children inclined to learn what is expected of them and of others merely by observing and by being a participating member of society. They will learn what it means to be a daughter, a son, a woman, a man, and the behaviors that go with these different roles. In the second case, persons are taught what to believe. They may be taught by their parents or at school, at church.

When it comes to attaining your objectives or creating change in your life if perhaps won't be simple. You may have to struggle. It will likely take a longer time period than you expect. It is almost certain that you will have short-term failures and setbacks along the way. Particularly when it involves developing new skills, forming a new resolution, creating new habits, or learning new concepts. Now, the good news, struggle, setbacks, battles, and short-term obstacles do not have to drain your motivation. They do not have to make you want to quit before you have put in enough effort and time to accomplish your goal. In fact, psychologists who study motivation and accomplishment say it could be just the opposite; as long as you adopt the right path and the right mindset. According to my raids of research through decades, there are two fundamental belief systems, also called as "mindsets," that evaluate how people respond to setbacks, struggle, obstacles, and failure when pursuing their goals. In one mindset, you are most likely to get discouraged and give up on your ultimate goal. In the other, you tend to embrace the battle and struggle, learn from the hardship or hurdles and keep moving forward to attain your goals– you persevere.

The science of Persistence: Determined Mindset vs Growth Mindset

What do you believe about human calibers, such as intelligence, talent, and creativeness? If you have adopted a "fixed mindset," you view them as traits that you are either born with, or not, and it is not much you can do to alter it. On the flip side, if you have adopted a "growth mindset," you see them as capacities that you can develop through determination, practice, education, and hard work.

How about character traits like grit, willpower, and self-discipline,? With a fixed mindset, you believe attributes like these are mostly static and predetermined by your genes and fostering – either you have them or you do not. Through the lens of a growth mindset, you see them as malleable skills that you can prepare, gear up and strengthen over the course of your life (even science also proves this to be true).

In a fixed mindset, people believe their basic attributes, like their intelligence, ability, or talent, are just fixed traits. They spend their time on the piece of writing their intelligence or talent instead of developing them. They also accept the fact that talent alone creates success; without excessive effort. They are actually wrong. On the flip side, in a growth mindset, people believe that their most basic qualities can be developed through dedication, commitment, and hard work. This view creates a love of learning and a resilience that is necessary for great achievement. Virtually all great people have had these calibers. Teaching a growth mindset creates productivity and motivation in the worlds of education, business, and sports. It deepens relationships. When you read Mindset, you will see how.

Fixed Mindset Weakens Your Dedication

Our mind is a meaning-making machine. Whether you are aware of it or not, you are continuously monitoring what is happening around you, understanding what it means and deciding what to do about it. This is apparently the significant procedure for your survival, but it is also the main driver of all your suffering – particularly when it is molded by the fixed mindset. When you struggle hardship or fail to attain your ultimate objectives, you make that mean something about yourself. In the fixed mindset, this mainly means you are simply not good enough, or that you for some reason do not have what it takes. For instance, have you ever thought or said things like: I'm not creative, I don't have any self-discipline, I have no talent, I'm not good with new technology, It's hard for me to lose the extra pound, I'm shy, I am not athletic, etc. It is healthy to acknowledge your limitations and recognize where you can be doing better in your life. But that's not what's happening in the fixed mindset. Remember, the fixed mindset believes that abilities and talent are mainly fixed and preset – either you have it, or don't. If you have, great. If not, why even why bother to try? You might as well give up, and keep move on to something simpler. Perhaps, this is not the kind of thinking that helped the big personalities like J.K. Rowling and Stephen King become bestselling authors. It is not the kind of thinking that creates motivation to persevere when the going gets tough.

Growth Mindset Fortifies Your Motivation

The growth mindset interprets failure and challenging situations much differently than the fixed mindset. Just remember, the core opinion of the growth mindset is that human powers and talents are malleable skills that you can set up and strengthen over the course of your life. The fixed mindset erroneously views your limitations as permanent. On the other hand, the growth mindset understands they are just a starting turning point – guiding stars that tell you where to spend your energy toward professional and personal development. The growth mindset is an antidote to defeatism. It interprets challenge & failure, not as a signal to throw in the towel, however, as a healthy and natural part of human growing and accomplishment.

This might sound like a good old-fashioned or outdated positive thinking, and maybe it is. The difference of opinion is these conclusions are based on 40 years of stringent, scientific research – more than hundreds of studies that all say the similar facts. If you want to strengthen your motivation, accomplish your goals and lead a more fulfilling life, you are best served by a growth mindset. You now have a choice with regard to how you interpret struggle, failure, and setbacks. You can interpret it from a fixed mindset as proof that you are somehow not cut out to win. Or you can interpret it from a growth mindset as guidance for where to keep your focus on your efforts toward personal & professional development. Most persistence research on naive theories has focused on beliefs about people and how they feel, behave, think, and interact and other social theories. Examples include stereotypes about teenagers, Muslims, Asian Americans; beliefs about artists, lawyers, firefighters; even beliefs about the causes of poverty, violence or war.

Early belief perseverance studies tested whether individuals often truly cling to unfounded viewpoints more so than is logically justifiable. However, it is complex and tricky to specify just how much a given belief "should" modify in response to fresh and new testament. One "C Grade" on a math test should not completely overwhelm other years of "A"s in other math classes, however, how much transform (if any) is warranted? There is one clear and apparent case in which researchers can state how much belief change should happen. That case is when the basis of a precise belief is totally dishonored or discredited. For instance, imagine that John tells Maria that the new team member is not very active. Maria may even meet and interact with the new member for several days before learning that John was actually speaking about a different new joiner. Because Maria knows that his initial belief about new member's intelligence was based on completely irrelevant information, Maria's impression about the new joiner should now be totally uninfluenced by John's initial statement. This, in essence, describes the debriefing paradigm, the primary technique used to study unwarranted belief perseverance. In the first belief perseverance revision using this way, partially half of the research participant members were led to suppose and believe that they had performed fine on a social perceptiveness task; the rest half were led to judge that they had performed badly. Afterward, all were told that their performance had been manipulated by the researcher to see how participant members take action and respond to failure or success. Participants were even shown the paper sheet that listed their name and whether they were thought to be given failure or success feedback. Later, participants had to guess how well they really did and foresee how well they would do in the future on this assigned task or job.

Logically, those in the initial failure and success situations should not differ in their self-beliefs about their future or actual performance on this social perceptiveness job, for the reason that early beliefs based on the fake feedback should revert to their normal level once it was exposed that the feedback was faked. Nevertheless, participants who received fake success feedback constantly believe that they were pretty good at this task, while those who received fake failure comment persistently believe that they were pretty bad at it. Other studies of social impressions and self-impressions have found parallel effects concerning distinct beliefs.

The initial study of social theory persistence used the same debriefing paradigm to find out whether fictitious info about the relation between the personality attribute "riskiness" and firefighter quality could create a perseverant social theory. Though, after debriefing about the fictitious nature of the first information, participants at the start led to believe that risky people make finer firefighters and those initially led to believe that high-risk people make poorer firefighters persist in their initial beliefs. At least there are three psychological procedures underlie belief perseverance. One refers to use of the "availability heuristic" for deciding what is most liable to happen. When judging your own power at a specific task, you are likely to try to recollect memory how good you have done on similar tasks in the past, that is, how available (in memory) are past successfulness versus failures. However, whether you recall more failures or successes critically depends on galore factors, such as how memorable the several occasions were and how often you have actually thought about them, but not inevitably on how often you have failed or succeeded. The second activity concerns "illusory correlation," wherein one sees or remembers more confirmative cases and few disconfirming cases than really subsist. The third procedure concerns "data distortions," wherein disconfirming cases are neglected and confirming cases are inadvertent. For instance, if you are told that a new team member is rude, you are more likely to treat that individual in a way that invites rudeness or discourtesy and to forget instances of politeness. Research also has examined ways or reducing belief perseverance. The most obvious answer, asking people to be unbiased, does not work. Nevertheless, various techniques to reduce the problem. The most successful is to get the individual to imagine or explain how the other belief might be true. This de-biasing technique is referred to as the counter explanation.

Varied Types

There are three extraordinary kinds of belief perseverance, viz.,

Social impressions

Self-impressions

Naive theories

Social Impressions

Social Impressions bring up to the beliefs that people have about others. These could be supported on a one-time, previous experience (either positive or negative) that people have about others and shape an opinion, which leads into forming an opinion. These can be formed with just about any individual.

Self-impressions

Self-impressions mentioning to the beliefs that we harbor about ourselves. These have to do with our belief about our confidence, athletic skills, body image, academic capableness, musical knowledge, and the like. This belief system considers both negative and positive beliefs. For instance, somebody might be a good public speaker, however, he/ she has a strong belief that he cannot speak in the public place, and it cannot be shaken in spite of people complimenting him. The mistaken belief like this one can have severe consequences and can lead to a skewed perspective of oneself.

On the other hand, an exaggerated view of someone can also lead to problems.

Naive Theories

Such impressions are based on someone's belief about how the world works. Naive theories mostly correspond with social theories—the belief about folks, how they behave, think, and interact with others. Naive theories go on to comprise major stereotypes steeped in the society that has to do with the handful of issues about communities, religion, teen, professions, and other beliefs that may even comprise what gives rise to poorness, causes of war, and violence, and the like.

CHAPTER2

How Belief Perseverance Affects Us?

Holding on to set beliefs and speculations based on unwarranted data and in the light of conflicting evidence, demonstrates that conviction persistence exists, as well as that our conviction framework isn't just shaped based on certainties and sensible data, however to an expansive degree on how we feel about ourselves, about others, and about other general theories and hypotheses. Despite the fact that this unwavering belief can help from numerous points of view, most different occasions, it shapes a boundary which keeps us from settling on the correct decisions. Illustration of a similar will be featured in the accompanying area.

Examples

Positive Example-You're a brilliant cook and individuals dependably compliment you on your dishes. Yet, on one specific event, you happen to burn the sandwich you're cooking; this does not imply that you're an awful cook or that you need to scrutinize your conviction about being a decent cook. For this situation, the belief perseverance has enabled you to restore your confidence in your cooking and continue.

Negative Examples-However, there are occasions when belief perseverance goes about as a hurdle. For instance, a man has met with 4 accidents during a span of a month, but, he keeps on trusting that he is a superb driver. Or then again suppose that your companion has been dating a person who treats her badly, and whilst everybody around her can see this and have been revealing to her the same, she basically declines to say a final breakup to him since she trusts he loves her as too, and he will change.

In the two instances, the individual does not take cognizance of anything that repudiates his/her belief system, which at that point negatively affects his life, since he can't take logical conclusion or judgment.

Do you believe in persistence?

Aren't you? Persistence is being able to continue an human action until one has succeeded, like winning a race. When you start running, you keep on pushing yourself until you have crossed the finish line. Or instance, in special education, having persistence in teaching a kid until he/she has reached their ultimate goal is like a race. You are persistent in helping them reach their destination and don't stop until they have reached their objective. People tend to hold on to their beliefs even when it seems that they should not. Persistence is the tendency to cling to one's initial belief even after receiving fresh information that dis-confirms or contradicts or the basis of that belief. Every single person has tried to change somebody's belief, only to have them obdurately remain unchanged. For example, you may have had such debates concerning the abortion, or evolution.

 In the plethora of cases, resistance to challenges to belies is defensible and logical. For instance, if you have always done well in racing, getting the third position on some race should not lead you to abandon your belief that you are generally good in the race. However, in the handful of cases, people cling to beliefs that logically should be abandoned, or at least altered. There is overpowering evidence that smoking increases the probability of contracting cancer and that exposure to media violence heightens the likelihood of aggressive behavior. Even, some people strongly deny these scientific facts. People expend considerable mental energy to maintain their opinion when presented with facts that prove them wrong. They will concentrate on experiences that support their point of view merely will ignore any experiences, even their own, that give grounds that they are wrong. They will do the same thing with any other kinds of evidence as well.

Types of Belief of Perseverance

There are three types of belief perseverance exist —1) social impressions 2)self-impressions, and 3) social theories. The first kind of belief consists of beliefs about the self, considering what one believes about his skills and abilities, including body image and social skills. The second type comprises one belief about specific others, for instance, a parent or best friend. The third type comprises mainly what one believes about how the world mainly works, comprising how people act, feel, interact and think. Social theory opinion can be either directly or indirectly learned which means that they can learn through experience as a member or they can be taught. In the first case, children inclined to learn what is expected of them and of others merely by observing and by being a participating member of society. They will learn what it means to be a daughter, a son, a woman, a man, and the behaviors that go with these different roles. In the second case, persons are taught what to believe. They may be taught by their parents or at school, at church.

When it comes to attaining your objectives or creating change in your life if perhaps won't be simple. You may have to struggle. It will likely take a longer time period than you expect. It is almost certain that you will have short-term failures and setbacks along the way. Particularly when it involves developing new skills, forming a new resolution, creating new habits, or learning new concepts. Now, the good news, struggle, setbacks, battles, and short-term obstacles do not have to drain your motivation. They do not have to make you want to quit before you have put in enough effort and time to accomplish your goal. In fact, psychologists who study motivation and accomplishment say it could be just the opposite; as long as you adopt the right path and the right mindset. According to my raids of research through decades, there are two fundamental belief systems, also called as "mindsets," that evaluate how people respond to setbacks, struggle, obstacles, and failure when pursuing their goals. In one mindset, you are most likely to get discouraged and give up on your ultimate goal. In the other, you tend to embrace the battle and struggle, learn from the hardship or hurdles and keep moving forward to attain your goals– you persevere.

The science of Persistence: Determined Mindset vs Growth Mindset

What do you believe about human calibers, such as intelligence, talent, and creativeness? If you have adopted a "fixed mindset," you view them as traits that you are either born with, or not, and it is not much you can do to alter it. On the flip side, if you have adopted a "growth mindset," you see them as capacities that you can develop through determination, practice, education, and hard work.

How about character traits like grit, willpower, and self-discipline,? With a fixed mindset, you believe attributes like these are mostly static and predetermined by your genes and fostering – either you have them or you do not. Through the lens of a growth mindset, you see them as malleable skills that you can prepare, gear up and strengthen over the course of your life (even science also proves this to be true).

In a fixed mindset, people believe their basic attributes, like their intelligence, ability, or talent, are just fixed traits. They spend their time on the piece of writing their intelligence or talent instead of developing them. They also accept the fact that talent alone creates success; without excessive effort. They are actually wrong. On the flip side, in a growth mindset, people believe that their most basic qualities can be developed through dedication, commitment, and hard work. This view creates a love of learning and a resilience that is necessary for great achievement. Virtually all great people have had these calibers. Teaching a growth mindset creates productivity and motivation in the worlds of education, business, and sports. It deepens relationships. When you read Mindset, you will see how.

Fixed Mindset Weakens Your Dedication

Our mind is a meaning-making machine. Whether you are aware of it or not, you are continuously monitoring what is happening around you, understanding what it means and deciding what to do about it. This is apparently the significant procedure for your survival, but it is also the main driver of all your suffering – particularly when it is molded by the fixed mindset. When you struggle hardship or fail to attain your ultimate objectives, you make that mean something about yourself. In the fixed mindset, this mainly means you are simply not good enough, or that you for some reason do not have what it takes. For instance, have you ever thought or said things like: I'm not creative, I don't have any self-discipline, I have no talent, I'm not good with new technology, It's hard for me to lose the extra pound, I'm shy, I am not athletic, etc. It is healthy to acknowledge your limitations and recognize where you can be doing better in your life. But that's not what's happening in the fixed mindset. Remember, the fixed mindset believes that abilities and talent are mainly fixed and preset – either you have it, or don't. If you have, great. If not, why even why bother to try? You might as well give up, and keep move on to something simpler. Perhaps, this is not the kind of thinking that helped the big personalities like J.K. Rowling and Stephen King become bestselling authors. It is not the kind of thinking that creates motivation to persevere when the going gets tough.

Growth Mindset Fortifies Your Motivation

The growth mindset interprets failure and challenging situations much differently than the fixed mindset. Just remember, the core opinion of the growth mindset is that human powers and talents are malleable skills that you can set up and strengthen over the course of your life. The fixed mindset erroneously views your limitations as permanent. On the other hand, the growth mindset understands they are just a starting turning point – guiding stars that tell you where to spend your energy toward professional and personal development. The growth mindset is an antidote to defeatism. It interprets challenge & failure, not as a signal to throw in the towel, however, as a healthy and natural part of human growing and accomplishment.

This might sound like a good old-fashioned or outdated positive thinking, and maybe it is. The difference of opinion is these conclusions are based on 40 years of stringent, scientific research – more than hundreds of studies that all say the similar facts. If you want to strengthen your motivation, accomplish your goals and lead a more fulfilling life, you are best served by a growth mindset. You now have a choice with regard to how you interpret struggle, failure, and setbacks. You can interpret it from a fixed mindset as proof that you are somehow not cut out to win. Or you can interpret it from a growth mindset as guidance for where to keep your focus on your efforts toward personal & professional development. Most persistence research on naive theories has focused on beliefs about people and how they feel, behave, think, and interact and other social theories. Examples include stereotypes about teenagers, Muslims, Asian Americans; beliefs about artists, lawyers, firefighters; even beliefs about the causes of poverty, violence or war.

Early belief perseverance studies tested whether individuals often truly cling to unfounded viewpoints more so than is logically justifiable. However, it is complex and tricky to specify just how much a given belief "should" modify in response to fresh and new testament. One "C Grade" on a math test should not completely overwhelm other years of "A"s in other math classes, however, how much transform (if any) is warranted? There is one clear and apparent case in which researchers can state how much belief change should happen. That case is when the basis of a precise belief is totally dishonored or discredited. For instance, imagine that John tells Mariah that the new team member is not very active. Mariah may even meet and interact with the new member for several days before learning that John was actually speaking about a different new joiner. Because Mariah knows that his initial belief about new member's intelligence was based on completely irrelevant information, Mariah's impression about the new joiner should now be totally uninfluenced by John's initial statement. This, in essence, describes the debriefing paradigm, the primary technique used to study unwarranted belief perseverance. In the first belief perseverance revision using this way, partially half of the research participant members were led to suppose and believe that they had performed fine on a social perceptiveness task; the rest half were led to judge that they had performed badly. Afterward, all were told that their performance had been manipulated by the researcher to see how participant members take action and respond to failure or success. Participants were even shown the paper sheet that listed their name and whether they were thought to be given failure or success feedback. Later, participants had to guess how well they really did and foresee how well they would do in the future on this assigned task or job.

Logically, those in the initial failure and success situations should not differ in their self-beliefs about their future or actual performance on this social perceptiveness job, for the reason that early beliefs based on the fake feedback should revert to their normal level once it was exposed that the feedback was faked. Nevertheless, participants who received fake success feedback constantly believe that they were pretty good at this task, while those who received fake failure comment persistently believe that they were pretty bad at it. Other studies of social impressions and self-impressions have found parallel effects concerning distinct beliefs.

 The initial study of social theory persistence used the same debriefing paradigm to find out whether fictitious info about the relation between the personality attribute "riskiness" and firefighter quality could create a perseverant social theory. Though, after debriefing about the fictitious nature of the first information, participants at the start led to believe that risky people make finer firefighters and those initially led to believe that high-risk people make poorer firefighters persist in their initial beliefs. At least there are three psychological procedures underlie belief perseverance. One refers to use of the "availability heuristic" for deciding what is most liable to happen. When judging your own power at a specific task, you are likely to try to recollect memory how good you have done on similar tasks in the past, that is, how available (in memory) are past successfulness versus failures. However, whether you recall more failures or successes critically depends on galore factors, such as how memorable the several occasions were and how often you have actually thought about them, but not inevitably on how often you have failed or succeeded. The second activity concerns "illusory correlation," wherein one sees or remembers more confirmative cases and few disconfirming cases than really subsist. The third procedure concerns "data distortions," wherein disconfirming cases are neglected and confirming cases are inadvertent. For instance, if you are told that a new team member is rude, you are more likely to treat that individual in a way that invites rudeness or discourtesy and to forget instances of politeness. Research also has examined ways or reducing belief perseverance. The most obvious answer, asking people to be unbiased, does not work. Nevertheless, various techniques to reduce the problem. The most successful is to get the individual to imagine or explain how the other belief might be true. This de-biasing technique is referred to as the counter explanation.

Varied Types

There are three extraordinary kinds of belief perseverance, viz.,

Social impressions

Self-impressions

Naive theories

Social Impressions

Social Impressions bring up to the beliefs that people have about others. These could be supported on a one-time, previous experience (either positive or negative) that people have about others and shape an opinion, which leads into forming an opinion. These can be formed with just about any individual.

Self-impressions

Self-impressions mentioning to the beliefs that we harbor about ourselves. These have to do with our belief about our confidence, athletic skills, body image, academic capableness, musical knowledge, and the like. This belief system considers both negative and positive beliefs. For instance, somebody might be a good public speaker, however, he/ she has a strong belief that he cannot speak in the public place, and it cannot be shaken in spite of people complimenting him. The mistaken belief like this one can have severe consequences and can lead to a skewed perspective of oneself. On the other hand, an exaggerated view of someone can also lead to problems.

Naive Theories

Such impressions are based on someone's belief about how the world works. Naive theories mostly correspond with social theories—the belief about folks, how they behave, think, and interact with others. Naive theories go on to comprise major stereotypes steeped in the society that has to do with the handful of issues about communities, religion, teen, professions, and other beliefs that may even comprise what gives rise to poorness, causes of war, and violence, and the like.

How Belief Perseverance Affects Us?

Holding on to set beliefs and speculations based on unwarranted data and in the light of conflicting evidence, demonstrates that conviction persistence exists, as well as that our conviction framework isn't just shaped based on certainties and sensible data, however to an expansive degree on how we feel about ourselves, about others, and about other general theories and hypotheses. Despite the fact that this unwavering belief can help from numerous points of view, most different occasions, it shapes a boundary which keeps us from settling on the correct decisions. Illustration of a similar will be featured in the accompanying area.

Examples

Positive Example-You're a brilliant cook and individuals dependably compliment you on your dishes. Yet, on one specific event, you happen to burn the sandwich you're cooking; this does not imply that you're an awful cook or that you need to scrutinize your conviction about being a decent cook. For this situation, the belief perseverance has enabled you to restore your confidence in your cooking and continue.

Negative Examples-However, there are occasions when belief perseverance goes about as a hurdle. For instance, a man has met with 4 accidents during a span of a month, but, he keeps on trusting that he is a superb driver. Or then again suppose that your companion has been dating a person who treats her badly, and whilst everybody around her can see this and have been revealing to her the same, she basically declines to say a final breakup to him since she trusts he loves her as too, and he will change.

In the two instances, the individual does not take cognizance of anything that repudiates his/her belief system, which at that point negatively affects his life, since he can't take logical conclusion or judgment.

Do you believe in persistence?

Aren't you? Persistence is being able to continue an human action until one has succeeded, like winning a race. When you start running, you keep on pushing yourself until you have crossed the finish line. Or instance, in special education, having persistence in teaching a kid until he/she has reached their ultimate goal is like a race. You are persistent in helping them reach their destination and don't stop until they have reached their objective. People tend to hold on to their beliefs even when it seems that they should not. Persistence is the tendency to cling to one's initial belief even after receiving fresh information that dis-confirms or contradicts or the basis of that belief. Every single person has tried to change somebody's belief, only to have them obdurately remain unchanged. For example, you may have had such debates concerning the abortion, or evolution.

In the plethora of cases, resistance to challenges to belies is defensible and logical. For instance, if you have always done well in racing, getting the third position on some race should not lead you to abandon your belief that you are generally good in the race. However, in the handful of cases, people cling to beliefs that logically should be abandoned, or at least altered. There is overpowering evidence that smoking increases the probability of contracting cancer and that exposure to media violence heightens the likelihood of aggressive behavior. Even, some people strongly deny these scientific facts. People expend considerable mental energy to maintain their opinion when presented with facts that prove them wrong. They will concentrate on experiences that support their point of view merely will ignore any experiences, even their own, that give grounds that they are wrong. They will do the same thing with any other kinds of evidence as well.

Types of Belief of Perseverance

There are three types of belief perseverance exist —1) social impressions 2)self-impressions, and 3) social theories. The first kind of belief consists of beliefs about the self, considering what one believes about his skills and abilities, including body image and social skills. The second type comprises one belief about specific others, for instance, a parent or best friend. The third type comprises mainly what one believes about how the world mainly works, comprising how people act, feel, interact and think. Social theory opinion can be either directly or indirectly learned which means that they can learn through experience as a member or they can be taught. In the first case, children inclined to learn what is expected of them and of others merely by observing and by being a participating member of society. They will learn what it means to be a daughter, a son, a woman, a man, and the behaviors that go with these different roles. In the second case, persons are taught what to believe. They may be taught by their parents or at school, at church.

When it comes to attaining your objectives or creating change in your life if perhaps won't be simple. You may have to struggle. It will likely take a longer time period than you expect. It is almost certain that you will have short-term failures and setbacks along the way. Particularly when it involves developing new skills, forming a new resolution, creating new habits, or learning new concepts. Now, the good news, struggle, setbacks, battles, and short-term obstacles do not have to drain your motivation. They do not have to make you want to quit before you have put in enough effort and time to accomplish your goal. In fact, psychologists who study motivation and accomplishment say it could be just the opposite; as long as you adopt the right path and the right mindset. According to my raids of research through decades, there are two fundamental belief systems, also called as "mindsets," that evaluate how people respond to setbacks, struggle, obstacles, and failure when pursuing their goals. In one mindset, you are most likely to get discouraged and give up on your ultimate goal. In the other, you tend to embrace the battle and struggle, learn from the hardship or hurdles and keep moving forward to attain your goals– you persevere.

The science of Persistence: Determined Mindset vs Growth Mindset

What do you believe about human calibers, such as intelligence, talent, and creativeness? If you have adopted a "fixed mindset," you view them as traits that you are either born with, or not, and it is not much you can do to alter it. On the flip side, if you have adopted a "growth mindset," you see them as capacities that you can develop through determination, practice, education, and hard work.

How about character traits like grit, willpower, and self-discipline,? With a fixed mindset, you believe attributes like these are mostly static and predetermined by your genes and fostering – either you have them or you do not. Through the lens of a growth mindset, you see them as malleable skills that you can prepare, gear up and strengthen over the course of your life (even science also proves this to be true).

In a fixed mindset, people believe their basic attributes, like their intelligence, ability, or talent, are just fixed traits. They spend their time on the piece of writing their intelligence or talent instead of developing them. They also accept the fact that talent alone creates success; without excessive effort. They are actually wrong. On the flip side, in a growth mindset, people believe that their most basic qualities can be developed through dedication, commitment, and hard work. This view creates a love of learning and a resilience that is necessary for great achievement. Virtually all great people have had these calibers.

CHAPTER3

Teaching a growth mindset creates productivity and motivation in the worlds of education, business, and sports. It deepens relationships. When you read Mindset, you will see how.

Fixed Mindset Weakens Your Dedication

Our mind is a meaning-making machine. Whether you are aware of it or not, you are continuously monitoring what is happening around you, understanding what it means and deciding what to do about it. This is apparently the significant procedure for your survival, but it is also the main driver of all your suffering – particularly when it is molded by the fixed mindset. When you struggle hardship or fail to attain your ultimate objectives, you make that mean something about yourself. In the fixed mindset, this mainly means you are simply not good enough, or that you for some reason do not have what it takes. For instance, have you ever thought or said things like: I'm not creative, I don't have any self-discipline, I have no talent, I'm not good with new technology, It's hard for me to lose the extra pound, I'm shy, I am not athletic, etc. It is healthy to acknowledge your limitations and recognize where you can be doing better in your life. But that's not what's happening in the fixed mindset. Remember, the fixed mindset believes that abilities and talent are mainly fixed and preset – either you have it, or don't. If you have, great. If not, why even why bother to try? You might as well give up, and keep move on to something simpler. Perhaps, this is not the kind of thinking that helped the big personalities like J.K. Rowling and Stephen King become bestselling authors. It is not the kind of thinking that creates motivation to persevere when the going gets tough.

Growth Mindset Fortifies Your Motivation

The growth mindset interprets failure and challenging situations much differently than the fixed mindset. Just remember, the core opinion of the growth mindset is that human powers and talents are malleable skills that you can set up and strengthen over the course of your life. The fixed mindset erroneously views your limitations as permanent. On the other hand, the growth mindset understands they are just a starting turning point – guiding stars that tell you where to spend your energy toward professional and personal development. The growth mindset is an antidote to defeatism. It interprets challenge & failure, not as a signal to throw in the towel, however, as a healthy and natural part of human growing and accomplishment.

This might sound like a good old-fashioned or outdated positive thinking, and maybe it is. The difference of opinion is these conclusions are based on 40 years of stringent, scientific research – more than hundreds of studies that all say the similar facts. If you want to strengthen your motivation, accomplish your goals and lead a more fulfilling life, you are best served by a growth mindset. You now have a choice with regard to how you interpret struggle, failure, and setbacks. You can interpret it from a fixed mindset as proof that you are somehow not cut out to win. Or you can interpret it from a growth mindset as guidance for where to keep your focus on your efforts toward personal & professional development. Most persistence research on naive theories has focused on beliefs about people and how they feel, behave, think, and interact and other social theories. Examples include stereotypes about teenagers, Muslims, Asian Americans; beliefs about artists, lawyers, firefighters; even beliefs about the causes of poverty, violence or war.

 Early belief perseverance studies tested whether individuals often truly cling to unfounded viewpoints more so than is logically justifiable. However, it is complex and tricky to specify just how much a given belief "should" modify in response to fresh and new testament. One "C Grade" on a math test should not completely overwhelm other years of "A"s in other math classes, however, how much transform (if any) is warranted? There is one clear and apparent case in which researchers can state how much belief change should happen. That case is when the basis of a precise belief is totally dishonored or discredited. For instance, imagine that John tells Mariah that the new team member is not very active. Mariah may even meet and interact with the new member for several days before learning that John was actually speaking about a different new joiner. Because Mariah knows that his initial belief about new member's intelligence was based on completely irrelevant information, Mariah's impression about the new joiner should now be totally uninfluenced by John's initial statement. This, in essence, describes the debriefing paradigm, the primary technique used to study unwarranted belief perseverance. In the first belief perseverance revision using this way, partially half of the research participant members were led to suppose and believe that they had performed fine on a social perceptiveness task; the rest half were led to judge that they had performed badly. Afterward, all were told that their performance had been manipulated by the researcher to see how participant members take action and respond to failure or success. Participants were even shown the paper sheet that listed their name and whether they were thought to be given failure or success feedback. Later, participants had to guess how well they really did and foresee how well they would do in the future on this assigned task or job.

Logically, those in the initial failure and success situations should not differ in their self-beliefs about their future or actual performance on this social perceptiveness job, for the reason that early beliefs based on the fake feedback should revert to their normal level once it was exposed that the feedback was faked. Nevertheless, participants who received fake success feedback constantly believe that they were pretty good at this task, while those who received fake failure comment persistently believe that they were pretty bad at it. Other studies of social impressions and self-impressions have found parallel effects concerning distinct beliefs.

The initial study of social theory persistence used the same debriefing paradigm to find out whether fictitious info about the relation between the personality attribute "riskiness" and firefighter quality could create a perseverant social theory. Though, after debriefing about the fictitious nature of the first information, participants at the start led to believe that risky people make finer firefighters and those initially led to believe that high-risk people make poorer firefighters persist in their initial beliefs. At least there are three psychological procedures underlie belief perseverance. One refers to use of the "availability heuristic" for deciding what is most liable to happen. When judging your own power at a specific task, you are likely to try to recollect memory how good you have done on similar tasks in the past, that is, how available (in memory) are past successfulness versus failures. However, whether you recall more failures or successes critically depends on galore factors, such as how memorable the several occasions were and how often you have actually thought about them, but not inevitably on how often you have failed or succeeded. The second activity concerns "illusory correlation," wherein one sees or remembers more confirmative cases and few disconfirming cases than really subsist. The third procedure concerns "data distortions," wherein disconfirming cases are neglected and confirming cases are inadvertent. For instance, if you are told that a new team member is rude, you are more likely to treat that individual in a way that invites rudeness or discourtesy and to forget instances of politeness. Research also has examined ways or reducing belief perseverance. The most obvious answer, asking people to be unbiased, does not work. Nevertheless, various techniques to reduce the problem. The most successful is to get the individual to imagine or explain how the other belief might be true. This de-biasing technique is referred to as the counter explanation.

Varied Types

There are three extraordinary kinds of belief perseverance, viz.,

Social impressions

Self-impressions

Naive theories

Social Impressions

Social Impressions bring up to the beliefs that people have about others. These could be supported on a one-time, previous experience (either positive or negative) that people have about others and shape an opinion, which leads into forming an opinion. These can be formed with just about any individual.

Self-impressions

Self-impressions mentioning to the beliefs that we harbor about ourselves. These have to do with our belief about our confidence, athletic skills, body image, academic capableness, musical knowledge, and the like. This belief system considers both negative and positive beliefs. For instance, somebody might be a good public speaker, however, he/ she has a strong belief that he cannot speak in the public place, and it cannot be shaken in spite of people complimenting him. The mistaken belief like this one can have severe consequences and can lead to a skewed perspective of oneself. On the other hand, an exaggerated view of someone can also lead to problems.

Naive Theories

Such impressions are based on someone's belief about how the world works. Naive theories mostly correspond with social theories—the belief about folks, how they behave, think, and interact with others. Naive theories go on to comprise major stereotypes steeped in the society that has to do with the handful of issues about communities, religion, teen, professions, and other beliefs that may even comprise what gives rise to poorness, causes of war, and violence, and the like.

How Belief Perseverance Affects Us?

Holding on to set beliefs and speculations based on unwarranted data and in the light of conflicting evidence, demonstrates that conviction persistence exists, as well as that our conviction framework isn't just shaped based on certainties and sensible data, however to an expansive degree on how we feel about ourselves, about others, and about other general theories and hypotheses. Despite the fact that this unwavering belief can help from numerous points of view, most different occasions, it shapes a boundary which keeps us from settling on the correct decisions. Illustration of a similar will be featured in the accompanying area.

Examples

Positive Example-You're a brilliant cook and individuals dependably compliment you on your dishes. Yet, on one specific event, you happen to burn the sandwich you're cooking; this does not imply that you're an awful cook or that you need to scrutinize your conviction about being a decent cook. For this situation, the belief perseverance has enabled you to restore your confidence in your cooking and continue.

Negative Examples-However, there are occasions when belief perseverance goes about as a hurdle. For instance, a man has met with 4 accidents during a span of a month, but, he keeps on trusting that he is a superb driver. Or then again suppose that your companion has been dating a person who treats her badly, and whilst everybody around her can see this and have been revealing to her the same, she basically declines to say a final breakup to him since she trusts he loves her as too, and he will change.

 In the two instances, the individual does not take cognizance of anything that repudiates his/her belief system, which at that point negatively affects his life, since he can't take logical conclusion or judgment.

Why Persistence significant in our Life?

Persistence is the essences of accelerating your prospects of being successful in a specific thing or accomplishing a specific objective, and it likewise can assist you with staying motivated and continue striving towards the one long haul objective you want to achieve. For instance, when you first started your company, you most likely had dreams of success and recognition. You were positive that sales were reaching to pour in, and you'd be busy creating a great deal of cash. When you truly operated your company, it most likely dawned upon you rather quickly that hopes, visions, and

dreams alone weren't sufficient. Starting a business taught you that being a business owner isn't as simple as you once thought it might be. In fact, it's a great deal of labor with little reward gained at the outset. This is the reason why business failure rates are thus high. Folks merely cannot overcome the roadblocks and demands that accompany entrepreneurship.

The one word that may be used to describe businessperson who succeeds at business ownership is 'persistent'. You need to be persistent if you would like to be ready to sustain your business through the challenges and hurdles of entrepreneurship and sooner or later reap the rewards of a successful business. The truth is that Entrepreneurship comes with loads of ups and downs. Typically it feels as if you expertise a lot of downs than ups as you're within the early stages of business development. This is often once your mental attitude needs to stay optimistic and tough if you're getting to go through the hardships of constructing your business. If you're presently having a tough time in your business, you'd get advantage from reading some quotes regarding persistence. These quotes can assist you to understand that you simply

aren't the sole one who has undergone troubles as a business owner. Others are through what you're presently going through and possibly abundantly worse. But, they still built successful businesses despite their hurdles as a result of they remained to persevere.

The definition of Persistence is once you are desperate to do one thing considerably and not permitting anyone or any troubles stop you for doing it. This definition couldn't be any length suitable which is what the beauty of determination is and why it's therefore vital for anyone to have. With zero determination, it can lead you to give up on the single thing that you just needed to try to due to the issue that you just faced with or what somebody else has same. Nobody ought to ever surrender on one thing that they really need to try to as a result of everybody can achieve something if they are willing to place in the work a strong mindset towards overcoming the particular challenge and overcoming people that disagree and create trouble and don't have your best interest to your life.

Why Persistence is significant than planning?

We are mysterious creatures. Anguish and hope can coexist and still create something astonishing. Perseverance is the ability to maintain action despite your feelings. It has a lot to do with your life's success and business success. It is considered as an omnipotent. An American politician Calvin Coolidge once stated "The slogan "press on" has solved and always will solve the troubles of the human race". Intelligence and ability cannot take the place of persistence. The worth of persistence comes from a visualization of the future that is so compelling you would give approx anything to make it factual or real. Persistence of action draws closer from the persistence of vision. When you are specifically clear about what you want in such a way that your vision does not change much, you will be more unfailing and persistentin your dealings. Hence, that consistency of action will produce consistency of outcomes. One favorite quote state that "no plan survives first contact with the enemy." We have learned this reality time and time again. Mike Tyson put it well when he stated, "Everybody has an arrangement until the

point when they get punched in the face." Regular arranging is basic to maintain a business yet we find that readiness and steadiness are significantly more imperative that the most ideal marketable strategy. Clear emergency courses of action were basic for mission achievement.

Here are reasons that being well-prepared and persistent to tackle life's obstruction is significant than trying to manage things out of your control.

Things do not generally go as planned, thus be ready when the inevitable obstruction or hurdles stand in your way. Whether you are the team member of the big-giant corporation or an entrepreneur growing a start-up, you have probably noticed that plans can change, and change often. But the enterprise has to be well-structured to remain dynamic, robust and strong. Good leaders must continue focused on what lays ahead for foreseeing potential blockage and adjust accordingly. Experiencing letdown along your path to accomplishment does not mean you failed. Failure generally occurs when you allow those experiences cause you to give up. Planning does not ensure

adaptableness. In the Teams, while doing fight dive training we had a saying, "Plan your dive, & dive your plan." Things can get confusing underwater in pitch blackness, however, when you start second guess yourself, it can snowball uncontrollable. That's why it is said, good old fashion common sense is also a great reserve and stand-in when your plan starts falling apart.

For companies, o be adapt and dynamic to external and internal forces pushing against them, they must have robust financials, nimble leadership, and a team with a shared sense of purpose. Planning does not identify unknowns. Persistence and obstinacy are what makes companies successful. The character is built during the third and fourth shots at attaining the goal. Not the first try. In trade, there are always myriads of things out of your control like the economy or your client's financial situations. But that's senseless reason to irritate and make kneejerk decisions. You just have to stay calm, cool and positive and try to keep moving. A great quote about persistence from Martin Luther King Jr. states that "If you can't fly you run if you can't run you walk if you can't walk you crawls. But no matter what, you keep moving forward."

Good plans are valueless without proper implementation. Plus flawless execution takes some practice. You can use up all the time in the world developing big plans for your business but if you do not brag the ability to perform on those plans you will surely fail. There also has to be buy-in across the board for organizations to be effectual at hitting their goals. Never discount the significance of having a proper plan and even better contingency strategies. But you need to keep in mind that if you spend proper time to make sure you have the capability to adapt as required, it won't feel like you are trying to steer a cruise ship when an iceberg placed in your pathway. It is perseverance that keeps you moving forward, having important goals are not achieved overnight, they necessitate, and no they demand patience, perseverance, and persistence. If you persistently take action, you will build momentum. "If Columbus had ever thought to turn back, no one would have blamed him. No one would have memorized him either."

In the face of challenge, perseverance ensures that we continue to take action towards the accomplishment of our

objective. As World's famous educationalist points out, this may require us to frequent adjustments to our tactics, until we achieve the objective.

"If you have an important point to make, don't try to be subtle or clever. Use a pile driver. Hit the point once. Then come back and hit it again. Then hit it a third time - a tremendous whack."— Winston S. Churchill

Reflecting on your objectives...

• Do you require amending the strategies you are using to archive your goal?

• Have you persevered toward you objective? Or have you perhaps given up too soon?

There are two mentalities: buckle down and achieve your objectives, or not bother since you likely won't succeed in any case. In spite of the fact that this may appear to be an oversimplification, we think this oblivious choice has an aggravating impact all through your life. In the event that you are in the camp of "making a decent attempt leads to achievement", you invest more energy, you take rejection in your stride (despite the

fact that regardless it harms), you get up every single time you fall, and you feel motivated to attempt and attempt and try again until you succeed. Whether it's a spelling bee or beginning your own organization: trusting you can accomplish something through diligent work is a critical element for success. Be in the other camp of "you won't succeed" paying little heed to what you do, there is an unequivocally negative example. You feel that whatever you do throughout everyday life, you presumably won't succeed in any case, so you don't feel inspired to attempt in any case. When you confront difficulties and hurdles, you see that as a sign that you will fail. When you are rejected, again you feel weak, powerless and unfortunate.

In psychology, there's an idea called "locus of control": an individual's conviction about how long they can control the events around them: do you take control of the things you can control, or do you blame external components for your prosperity or disappointment. Sooner or later the vast majority have most likely identified with both camps. However, we imagine that over the time goes there is a huge exacerbating impact, encountering little hurdles and

difficulties and after that success, which inspires you to handle bigger challenges and to feel well prepared for greater misfortunes.

Set your psyche to an objective, something that you believe is bizarre and afterward buckles down to accomplish it. Depending upon the "challenge" you pick – it might take the number of hours or only a week. Learn a language, run more distant than you might suspect you could, and figure out how to cook another dish, get the courage to complete an open talking in Public, climb a mountain, build something, influence something, and create something. Set an objective that scares you a little and drives you out of your comfort zone. The truth is that you have accomplished something that you thought was unimaginable and not possible, you will be raring to go for your next toughest challenge and more resilient to the hindrances that you will unavoidably face out and along the way.

Here are 4 reasons Perseverance is vital to your prosperity and success:

1. PERSEVERANCE HELPS YOU CONQUER THE UNEXPECTED

At the point when things don't work out as expected, it's tempting to surrender. We lose

our confidence and consider moving onward to something that is less demanding. This is actually what the vast majorities of people do on the grounds that we're anxious about disappointment or failure and evade far from things that are hard and necessary. Plans make us feel safe, yet be prepared when things turn out of your control so you can land on your feet. You may need to change course and adjust somehow. Your objective continues to be the same as before, however, your roadmap may need to be changed. Try to develop a nimble mentality by attempting to anticipate potential misfortunes and have an alternate course of action for them.

2. PERSEVERANCE ENABLES YOU TO KEEP FOCUSED

At the point when things turn out badly, it is difficult to keep up motivation and core interest. Perseverance enables you to stay concentrated on long haul objectives so you can change your behavior accordingly. Regularly, this expects you to hold feelings in line to keep emotions in check from sabotaging your endeavors and efforts to continue advancing and moving forward. Visualize yourself achieving your objective regardless of what it takes. Watch out for

the objective and see yourself reaching the end.

3. PERSEVERANCE IS FED BY ENCOURAGEMENT AND SUPPORT

At the point when things turn out of your control, discover support and encouragement from people around you whom you trust and respect. In view of their experience and ability, search out their recommendation, suggestions, and proposals on the how to proficiently continue moving ahead. Successful individuals with perseverance comprehend that still need to do the tough work, yet it is extremely encouraging when you are surrounded with positive back up. Nobody is their very own island and we as a whole need other individuals' assistance and support. It may be a short talk or a couple of words of assistance. Be the individual who connects when you require assistance rather than to surrender. Do not be afraid to share your situations with other people, however, be particular about it. Ensure they are individuals who really need what is best for you and will give you both valuable and positive feedback. Seek for "mirror" companions or friends who will be fair, cherishing, honest, and objective.

4. PERSEVERANCE MAKES YOU DIG DEEP DOWN

If you are on a path that has meaning, value, and significance for you, you are unquestionably on the right path, so keep going. If you are not, then a delay or failure will be enough to make you surrender and try something else. Success can be exceptionally misleading on the grounds that frequently it is the place we remain, regardless of whether it's what truly fills us or not. It is a success that is based in complacency because we are too scared of failure to pursue the type of work that would offer worth and meaning. Don't take the easiest path, dig deep down where it counts and discovers the things that you can't leave; that are your true north. When you are pursuing that sort of objective, it won't make any difference what other individuals say on the grounds that your inner vision is far stronger than any external hindrance you will come up against.

Taking everything into account, in short, persistence is an essential piece of life. Its isolates the complete from the incomplete and just to recap, here are the 5 key reasons why having perseverance satisfies:

• Most successful persons have failed in any event once

• People jump at the chance to test you on the determination

• What comes effectively typically isn't justified, despite any potential benefits

• Knowledge isn't picked up without ingenuity and persistence

• The more you accomplish something, the better you get at it

Permanence, perseverance, and persistence in spite of all obstacles, discouragements, and impossibilities: It is this that in all things distinguishes the strong soul from the weak.

Why Persistence significant in our Life?

Persistence is the essences of accelerating your prospects of being successful in a specific thing or accomplishing a specific objective, and it likewise can assist you with staying motivated and continue striving towards the one long haul objective you want to achieve. For instance, when you first started your company, you most likely had dreams of success and recognition. You were positive that sales were reaching to pour in, and you'd be busy creating a great deal of cash. When you truly operated your company, it most likely dawned upon you rather quickly that hopes, visions, and

dreams alone weren't sufficient. Starting a business taught you that being a business owner isn't as simple as you once thought it might be. In fact, it's a great deal of labor with little reward gained at the outset. This is the reason why business failure rates are thus high. Folks merely cannot overcome the roadblocks and demands that accompany entrepreneurship.

The one word that may be used to describe businessperson who succeeds at business ownership is 'persistent'. You need to be persistent if you would like to be ready to sustain your business through the challenges and hurdles of entrepreneurship and sooner or later reap the rewards of a successful business. The truth is that Entrepreneurship comes with loads of ups and downs. Typically it feels as if you expertise a lot of downs than ups as you're within the early stages of business development. This is often once your mental attitude needs to stay optimistic and tough if you're getting to go through the hardships of constructing your business. If you're presently having a tough time in your business, you'd get advantage from reading some quotes regarding persistence. These quotes can assist you to understand that you simply

aren't the sole one who has undergone troubles as a business owner. Others are through what you're presently going through and possibly abundantly worse. But, they still built successful businesses despite their hurdles as a result of they remained to persevere.

The definition of Persistence is once you are desperate to do one thing considerably and not permitting anyone or any troubles stop you for doing it. This definition couldn't be any length suitable which is what the beauty of determination is and why it's therefore vital for anyone to have. With zero determination, it can lead you to give up on the single thing that you just needed to try to due to the issue that you just faced with or what somebody else has same. Nobody ought to ever surrender on one thing that they really need to try to as a result of everybody can achieve something if they are willing to place in the work a strong mindset towards overcoming the particular challenge and overcoming people that disagree and create trouble and don't have your best interest to your life.

Why Persistence is significant than planning?

We are mysterious creatures. Anguish and hope can coexist and still create something astonishing. Perseverance is the ability to maintain action despite your feelings. It has a lot to do with your life's success and business success. It is considered as an omnipotent. An American politician Calvin Coolidge once stated "The slogan "press on" has solved and always will solve the troubles of the human race". Intelligence and ability cannot take the place of persistence. The worth of persistence comes from a visualization of the future that is so compelling you would give approx anything to make it factual or real. Persistence of action draws closer from the persistence of vision. When you are specifically clear about what you want in such a way that your vision does not change much, you will be more unfailing and persistentin your dealings. Hence, that consistency of action will produce consistency of outcomes. One favorite quote state that "no plan survives first contact with the enemy." We have learned this reality time and time again. Mike Tyson put it well when he stated, "Everybody has an arrangement until the

point when they get punched in the face." Regular arranging is basic to maintain a business yet we find that readiness and steadiness are significantly more imperative that the most ideal marketable strategy. Clear emergency courses of action were basic for mission achievement.

Here are reasons that being well-prepared and persistent to tackle life's obstruction is significant than trying to manage things out of your control.

Things do not generally go as planned, thus be ready when the inevitable obstruction or hurdles stand in your way. Whether you are the team member of the big-giant corporation or an entrepreneur growing a start-up, you have probably noticed that plans can change, and change often. But the enterprise has to be well-structured to remain dynamic, robust and strong. Good leaders must continue focused on what lays ahead for foreseeing potential blockage and adjust accordingly. Experiencing letdown along your path to accomplishment does not mean you failed. Failure generally occurs when you allow those experiences cause you to give up. Planning does not ensure

adaptableness. In the Teams, while doing fight dive training we had a saying, "Plan your dive, & dive your plan." Things can get confusing underwater in pitch blackness, however, when you start second guess yourself, it can snowball uncontrollable. That's why it is said, good old fashion common sense is also a great reserve and stand-in when your plan starts falling apart.

For companies, o be adapt and dynamic to external and internal forces pushing against them, they must have robust financials, nimble leadership, and a team with a shared sense of purpose. Planning does not identify unknowns. Persistence and obstinacy are what makes companies successful. The character is built during the third and fourth shots at attaining the goal. Not the first try. In trade, there are always myriads of things out of your control like the economy or your client's financial situations. But that's senseless reason to irritate and make kneejerk decisions. You just have to stay calm, cool and positive and try to keep moving. A great quote about persistence from Martin Luther King Jr. states that "If you can't fly you run if you can't run you walk if you can't walk you crawls. But no matter what, you keep moving forward."

Good plans are valueless without proper implementation. Plus flawless execution takes some practice. You can use up all the time in the world developing big plans for your business but if you do not brag the ability to perform on those plans you will surely fail. There also has to be buy-in across the board for organizations to be effectual at hitting their goals. Never discount the significance of having a proper plan and even better contingency strategies. But you need to keep in mind that if you spend proper time to make sure you have the capability to adapt as required, it won't feel like you are trying to steer a cruise ship when an iceberg placed in your pathway. It is perseverance that keeps you moving forward, having important goals are not achieved overnight, they necessitate, and no they demand patience, perseverance, and persistence. If you persistently take action, you will build momentum. "If Columbus had ever thought to turn back, no one would have blamed him. No one would have memorized him either."

In the face of challenge, perseverance ensures that we continue to take action towards the accomplishment of our

objective. As World's famous educationalist points out, this may require us to frequent adjustments to our tactics, until we achieve the objective.

"If you have an important point to make, don't try to be subtle or clever. Use a pile driver. Hit the point once. Then come back and hit it again. Then hit it a third time - a tremendous whack."— Winston S. Churchill

Reflecting on your objectives...

• Do you require amending the strategies you are using to archive your goal?

• Have you persevered toward you objective? Or have you perhaps given up too soon?

There are two mentalities: buckle down and achieve your objectives, or not bother since you likely won't succeed in any case. In spite of the fact that this may appear to be an oversimplification, we think this oblivious choice has an aggravating impact all through your life. In the event that you are in the camp of "making a decent attempt leads to achievement", you invest more energy, you take rejection in your stride (despite the

fact that regardless it harms), you get up every single time you fall, and you feel motivated to attempt and attempt and try again until you succeed. Whether it's a spelling bee or beginning your own organization: trusting you can accomplish something through diligent work is a critical element for success. Be in the other camp of "you won't succeed" paying little heed to what you do, there is an unequivocally negative example. You feel that whatever you do throughout everyday life, you presumably won't succeed in any case, so you don't feel inspired to attempt in any case. When you confront difficulties and hurdles, you see that as a sign that you will fail. When you are rejected, again you feel weak, powerless and unfortunate.

In psychology, there's an idea called "locus of control": an individual's conviction about how long they can control the events around them: do you take control of the things you can control, or do you blame external components for your prosperity or disappointment. Sooner or later the vast majority have most likely identified with both camps. However, we imagine that over the time goes there is a huge exacerbating impact, encountering little hurdles and

difficulties and after that success, which inspires you to handle bigger challenges and to feel well prepared for greater misfortunes.

Set your psyche to an objective, something that you believe is bizarre and afterward buckles down to accomplish it. Depending upon the "challenge" you pick – it might take the number of hours or only a week. Learn a language, run more distant than you might suspect you could, and figure out how to cook another dish, get the courage to complete an open talking in Public, climb a mountain, build something, influence something, and create something. Set an objective that scares you a little and drives you out of your comfort zone. The truth is that you have accomplished something that you thought was unimaginable and not possible, you will be raring to go for your next toughest challenge and more resilient to the hindrances that you will unavoidably face out and along the way.

Here are 4 reasons Perseverance is vital to your prosperity and success:

1. PERSEVERANCE HELPS YOU CONQUER THE UNEXPECTED

At the point when things don't work out as expected, it's tempting to surrender. We lose

our confidence and consider moving onward to something that is less demanding. This is actually what the vast majorities of people do on the grounds that we're anxious about disappointment or failure and evade far from things that are hard and necessary. Plans make us feel safe, yet be prepared when things turn out of your control so you can land on your feet. You may need to change course and adjust somehow. Your objective continues to be the same as before, however, your roadmap may need to be changed. Try to develop a nimble mentality by attempting to anticipate potential misfortunes and have an alternate course of action for them.

2. PERSEVERANCE ENABLES YOU TO KEEP FOCUSED

At the point when things turn out badly, it is difficult to keep up motivation and core interest. Perseverance enables you to stay concentrated on long haul objectives so you can change your behavior accordingly. Regularly, this expects you to hold feelings in line to keep emotions in check from sabotaging your endeavors and efforts to continue advancing and moving forward. Visualize yourself achieving your objective regardless of what it takes. Watch out for

the objective and see yourself reaching the end.

3.   PERSEVERANCE   IS   FED   BY ENCOURAGEMENT AND SUPPORT

At the point when things turn out of your control, discover support and encouragement from people around you whom you trust and respect. In view of their experience and ability, search out their recommendation, suggestions, and proposals on the how to proficiently continue moving ahead. Successful individuals with perseverance comprehend that still need to do the tough work, yet it is extremely encouraging when you are surrounded with positive back up. Nobody is their very own island and we as a whole need other individuals' assistance and support. It may be a short talk or a couple of words of assistance. Be the individual who connects when you require assistance rather than to surrender. Do not be afraid to share your situations with other people, however, be particular about it. Ensure they are individuals who really need what is best for you and will give you both valuable and positive feedback. Seek for "mirror" companions or friends who will be fair, cherishing, honest, and objective.

4. PERSEVERANCE MAKES YOU DIG DEEP DOWN

If you are on a path that has meaning, value, and significance for you, you are unquestionably on the right path, so keep going. If you are not, then a delay or failure will be enough to make you surrender and try something else. Success can be exceptionally misleading on the grounds that frequently it is the place we remain, regardless of whether it's what truly fills us or not. It is a success that is based in complacency because we are too scared of failure to pursue the type of work that would offer worth and meaning. Don't take the easiest path, dig deep down where it counts and discovers the things that you can't leave; that are your true north. When you are pursuing that sort of objective, it won't make any difference what other individuals say on the grounds that your inner vision is far stronger than any external hindrance you will come up against.

Taking everything into account, in short, persistence is an essential piece of life. Its isolates the complete from the incomplete and just to recap, here are the 5 key reasons why having perseverance satisfies:

• Most successful persons have failed in any event once

- People jump at the chance to test you on the determination

- What comes effectively typically isn't justified, despite any potential benefits

- Knowledge isn't picked up without ingenuity and persistence

- The more you accomplish something, the better you get at it

Permanence, perseverance, and persistence in spite of all obstacles, discouragements, and impossibilities: It is this that in all things distinguishes the strong soul from the weak.

Why Persistence significant in our Life?

Persistence is the essences of accelerating your prospects of being successful in a specific thing or accomplishing a specific objective, and it likewise can assist you with staying motivated and continue striving towards the one long haul objective you want to achieve. For instance, when you first started your company, you most likely had dreams of success and recognition. You were positive that sales were reaching to pour in, and you'd be busy creating a great deal of cash. When you truly operated your company, it most likely dawned upon you rather quickly that hopes, visions, and

dreams alone weren't sufficient. Starting a business taught you that being a business owner isn't as simple as you once thought it might be. In fact, it's a great deal of labor with little reward gained at the outset. This is the reason why business failure rates are thus high. Folks merely cannot overcome the roadblocks and demands that accompany entrepreneurship.

The one word that may be used to describe businessperson who succeeds at business ownership is 'persistent'. You need to be persistent if you would like to be ready to sustain your business through the challenges and hurdles of entrepreneurship and sooner or later reap the rewards of a successful business. The truth is that Entrepreneurship comes with loads of ups and downs. Typically it feels as if you expertise a lot of downs than ups as you're within the early stages of business development. This is often once your mental attitude needs to stay optimistic and tough if you're getting to go through the hardships of constructing your business. If you're presently having a tough time in your business, you'd get advantage from reading some quotes regarding persistence. These quotes can assist you to understand that you simply

aren't the sole one who has undergone troubles as a business owner. Others are through what you're presently going through and possibly abundantly worse. But, they still built successful businesses despite their hurdles as a result of they remained to persevere.

The definition of Persistence is once you are desperate to do one thing considerably and not permitting anyone or any troubles stop you for doing it. This definition couldn't be any length suitable which is what the beauty of determination is and why it's therefore vital for anyone to have. With zero determination, it can lead you to give up on the single thing that you just needed to try to due to the issue that you just faced with or what somebody else has same. Nobody ought to ever surrender on one thing that they really need to try to as a result of everybody can achieve something if they are willing to place in the work a strong mindset towards overcoming the particular challenge and overcoming people that disagree and create trouble and don't have your best interest to your life.

Why Persistence is significant than planning?

We are mysterious creatures. Anguish and hope can coexist and still create something astonishing. Perseverance is the ability to maintain action despite your feelings. It has a lot to do with your life's success and business success. It is considered as an omnipotent. An American politician Calvin Coolidge once stated "The slogan "press on" has solved and always will solve the troubles of the human race". Intelligence and ability cannot take the place of persistence. The worth of persistence comes from a visualization of the future that is so compelling you would give approx anything to make it factual or real. Persistence of action draws closer from the persistence of vision. When you are specifically clear about what you want in such a way that your vision does not change much, you will be more unfailing and persistentin your dealings. Hence, that consistency of action will produce consistency of outcomes. One favorite quote state that "no plan survives first contact with the enemy." We have learned this reality time and time again. Mike Tyson put it well when he stated, "Everybody has an arrangement until the

point when they get punched in the face." Regular arranging is basic to maintain a business yet we find that readiness and steadiness are significantly more imperative that the most ideal marketable strategy. Clear emergency courses of action were basic for mission achievement.

Here are reasons that being well-prepared and persistent to tackle life's obstruction is significant than trying to manage things out of your control.

Things do not generally go as planned, thus be ready when the inevitable obstruction or hurdles stand in your way. Whether you are the team member of the big-giant corporation or an entrepreneur growing a start-up, you have probably noticed that plans can change, and change often. But the enterprise has to be well-structured to remain dynamic, robust and strong. Good leaders must continue focused on what lays ahead for foreseeing potential blockage and adjust accordingly. Experiencing letdown along your path to accomplishment does not mean you failed. Failure generally occurs when you allow those experiences cause you to give up. Planning does not ensure

adaptableness. In the Teams, while doing fight dive training we had a saying, "Plan your dive, & dive your plan." Things can get confusing underwater in pitch blackness, however, when you start second guess yourself, it can snowball uncontrollable. That's why it is said, good old fashion common sense is also a great reserve and stand-in when your plan starts falling apart.

For companies, o be adapt and dynamic to external and internal forces pushing against them, they must have robust financials, nimble leadership, and a team with a shared sense of purpose. Planning does not identify unknowns. Persistence and obstinacy are what makes companies successful. The character is built during the third and fourth shots at attaining the goal. Not the first try. In trade, there are always myriads of things out of your control like the economy or your client's financial situations. But that's senseless reason to irritate and make kneejerk decisions. You just have to stay calm, cool and positive and try to keep moving. A great quote about persistence from Martin Luther King Jr. states that "If you can't fly you run if you can't run you walk if you can't walk you crawls. But no matter what, you keep moving forward."

Good plans are valueless without proper implementation. Plus flawless execution takes some practice. You can use up all the time in the world developing big plans for your business but if you do not brag the ability to perform on those plans you will surely fail. There also has to be buy-in across the board for organizations to be effectual at hitting their goals. Never discount the significance of having a proper plan and even better contingency strategies. But you need to keep in mind that if you spend proper time to make sure you have the capability to adapt as required, it won't feel like you are trying to steer a cruise ship when an iceberg placed in your pathway. It is perseverance that keeps you moving forward, having important goals are not achieved overnight, they necessitate, and no they demand patience, perseverance, and persistence. If you persistently take action, you will build momentum. "If Columbus had ever thought to turn back, no one would have blamed him. No one would have memorized him either."

In the face of challenge, perseverance ensures that we continue to take action towards the accomplishment of our

objective. As World's famous educationalist points out, this may require us to frequent adjustments to our tactics, until we achieve the objective.

"If you have an important point to make, don't try to be subtle or clever. Use a pile driver. Hit the point once. Then come back and hit it again. Then hit it a third time - a tremendous whack."— Winston S. Churchill

Reflecting on your objectives...

• Do you require amending the strategies you are using to archive your goal?

• Have you persevered toward you objective? Or have you perhaps given up too soon?

There are two mentalities: buckle down and achieve your objectives, or not bother since you likely won't succeed in any case. In spite of the fact that this may appear to be an oversimplification, we think this oblivious choice has an aggravating impact all through your life. In the event that you are in the camp of "making a decent attempt leads to achievement", you invest more energy, you take rejection in your stride (despite the

fact that regardless it harms), you get up every single time you fall, and you feel motivated to attempt and attempt and try again until you succeed. Whether it's a spelling bee or beginning your own organization: trusting you can accomplish something through diligent work is a critical element for success. Be in the other camp of "you won't succeed" paying little heed to what you do, there is an unequivocally negative example. You feel that whatever you do throughout everyday life, you presumably won't succeed in any case, so you don't feel inspired to attempt in any case. When you confront difficulties and hurdles, you see that as a sign that you will fail. When you are rejected, again you feel weak, powerless and unfortunate.

In psychology, there's an idea called "locus of control": an individual's conviction about how long they can control the events around them: do you take control of the things you can control, or do you blame external components for your prosperity or disappointment. Sooner or later the vast majority have most likely identified with both camps. However, we imagine that over the time goes there is a huge exacerbating impact, encountering little hurdles and

difficulties and after that success, which inspires you to handle bigger challenges and to feel well prepared for greater misfortunes.

Set your psyche to an objective, something that you believe is bizarre and afterward buckles down to accomplish it. Depending upon the "challenge" you pick – it might take the number of hours or only a week. Learn a language, run more distant than you might suspect you could, and figure out how to cook another dish, get the courage to complete an open talking in Public, climb a mountain, build something, influence something, and create something. Set an objective that scares you a little and drives you out of your comfort zone. The truth is that you have accomplished something that you thought was unimaginable and not possible, you will be raring to go for your next toughest challenge and more resilient to the hindrances that you will unavoidably face out and along the way.

Here are 4 reasons Perseverance is vital to your prosperity and success:

1. PERSEVERANCE HELPS YOU CONQUER THE UNEXPECTED

At the point when things don't work out as expected, it's tempting to surrender. We lose

our confidence and consider moving onward to something that is less demanding. This is actually what the vast majorities of people do on the grounds that we're anxious about disappointment or failure and evade far from things that are hard and necessary. Plans make us feel safe, yet be prepared when things turn out of your control so you can land on your feet. You may need to change course and adjust somehow. Your objective continues to be the same as before, however, your roadmap may need to be changed. Try to develop a nimble mentality by attempting to anticipate potential misfortunes and have an alternate course of action for them.

2. PERSEVERANCE ENABLES YOU TO KEEP FOCUSED

At the point when things turn out badly, it is difficult to keep up motivation and core interest. Perseverance enables you to stay concentrated on long haul objectives so you can change your behavior accordingly. Regularly, this expects you to hold feelings in line to keep emotions in check from sabotaging your endeavors and efforts to continue advancing and moving forward. Visualize yourself achieving your objective regardless of what it takes. Watch out for

the objective and see yourself reaching the end.

3. PERSEVERANCE IS FED BY ENCOURAGEMENT AND SUPPORT

At the point when things turn out of your control, discover support and encouragement from people around you whom you trust and respect. In view of their experience and ability, search out their recommendation, suggestions, and proposals on the how to proficiently continue moving ahead. Successful individuals with perseverance comprehend that still need to do the tough work, yet it is extremely encouraging when you are surrounded with positive back up. Nobody is their very own island and we as a whole need other individuals' assistance and support. It may be a short talk or a couple of words of assistance. Be the individual who connects when you require assistance rather than to surrender. Do not be afraid to share your situations with other people, however, be particular about it. Ensure they are individuals who really need what is best for you and will give you both valuable and positive feedback. Seek for "mirror" companions or friends who will be fair, cherishing, honest, and objective.

4. PERSEVERANCE MAKES YOU DIG DEEP DOWN

If you are on a path that has meaning, value, and significance for you, you are unquestionably on the right path, so keep going. If you are not, then a delay or failure will be enough to make you surrender and try something else. Success can be exceptionally misleading on the grounds that frequently it is the place we remain, regardless of whether it's what truly fills us or not. It is a success that is based in complacency because we are too scared of failure to pursue the type of work that would offer worth and meaning. Don't take the easiest path, dig deep down where it counts and discovers the things that you can't leave; that are your true north. When you are pursuing that sort of objective, it won't make any difference what other individuals say on the grounds that your inner vision is far stronger than any external hindrance you will come up against.

Taking everything into account, in short, persistence is an essential piece of life. Its isolates the complete from the incomplete and just to recap, here are the 5 key reasons why having perseverance satisfies:

• Most successful persons have failed in any event once

• People jump at the chance to test you on the determination

• What comes effectively typically isn't justified, despite any potential benefits

• Knowledge isn't picked up without ingenuity and persistence

• The more you accomplish something, the better you get at it

Permanence, perseverance, and persistence in spite of all obstacles, discouragements, and impossibilities: It is this that in all things distinguishes the strong soul from the weak. Why Persistence significant in our Life?

Persistence is the essences of accelerating your prospects of being successful in a specific thing or accomplishing a specific objective, and it likewise can assist you with staying motivated and continue striving towards the one long haul objective you want to achieve. For instance, when you first started your company, you most likely had dreams of success and recognition. You were positive that sales were reaching to pour in, and you'd be busy creating a great deal of cash. When you truly operated your company, it most likely dawned upon you rather quickly that hopes, visions, and

dreams alone weren't sufficient. Starting a business taught you that being a business owner isn't as simple as you once thought it might be. In fact, it's a great deal of labor with little reward gained at the outset. This is the reason why business failure rates are thus high. Folks merely cannot overcome the roadblocks and demands that accompany entrepreneurship.

The one word that may be used to describe businessperson who succeeds at business ownership is 'persistent'. You need to be persistent if you would like to be ready to sustain your business through the challenges and hurdles of entrepreneurship and sooner or later reap the rewards of a successful business. The truth is that Entrepreneurship comes with loads of ups and downs. Typically it feels as if you expertise a lot of downs than ups as you're within the early stages of business development. This is often once your mental attitude needs to stay optimistic and tough if you're getting to go through the hardships of constructing your business. If you're presently having a tough time in your business, you'd get advantage from reading some quotes regarding persistence. These quotes can assist you to understand that you simply

aren't the sole one who has undergone troubles as a business owner. Others are through what you're presently going through and possibly abundantly worse. But, they still built successful businesses despite their hurdles as a result of they remained to persevere.

The definition of Persistence is once you are desperate to do one thing considerably and not permitting anyone or any troubles stop you for doing it. This definition couldn't be any length suitable which is what the beauty of determination is and why it's therefore vital for anyone to have. With zero determination, it can lead you to give up on the single thing that you just needed to try to due to the issue that you just faced with or what somebody else has same. Nobody ought to ever surrender on one thing that they really need to try to as a result of everybody can achieve something if they are willing to place in the work a strong mindset towards overcoming the particular challenge and overcoming people that disagree and create trouble and don't have your best interest to your life.

Why Persistence is significant than planning?

We are mysterious creatures. Anguish and hope can coexist and still create something astonishing. Perseverance is the ability to maintain action despite your feelings. It has a lot to do with your life's success and business success. It is considered as an omnipotent. An American politician Calvin Coolidge once stated "The slogan "press on" has solved and always will solve the troubles of the human race". Intelligence and ability cannot take the place of persistence. The worth of persistence comes from a visualization of the future that is so compelling you would give approx anything to make it factual or real. Persistence of action draws closer from the persistence of vision. When you are specifically clear about what you want in such a way that your vision does not change much, you will be more unfailing and persistentin your dealings. Hence, that consistency of action will produce consistency of outcomes. One favorite quote state that "no plan survives first contact with the enemy." We have learned this reality time and time again. Mike Tyson put it well when he stated, "Everybody has an arrangement until the

point when they get punched in the face." Regular arranging is basic to maintain a business yet we find that readiness and steadiness are significantly more imperative that the most ideal marketable strategy. Clear emergency courses of action were basic for mission achievement.

Here are reasons that being well-prepared and persistent to tackle life's obstruction is significant than trying to manage things out of your control.

Things do not generally go as planned, thus be ready when the inevitable obstruction or hurdles stand in your way. Whether you are the team member of the big-giant corporation or an entrepreneur growing a start-up, you have probably noticed that plans can change, and change often. But the enterprise has to be well-structured to remain dynamic, robust and strong. Good leaders must continue focused on what lays ahead for foreseeing potential blockage and adjust accordingly. Experiencing letdown along your path to accomplishment does not mean you failed. Failure generally occurs when you allow those experiences cause you to give up. Planning does not ensure

adaptableness. In the Teams, while doing fight dive training we had a saying, "Plan your dive, & dive your plan." Things can get confusing underwater in pitch blackness, however, when you start second guess yourself, it can snowball uncontrollable. That's why it is said, good old fashion common sense is also a great reserve and stand-in when your plan starts falling apart.

For companies, o be adapt and dynamic to external and internal forces pushing against them, they must have robust financials, nimble leadership, and a team with a shared sense of purpose. Planning does not identify unknowns. Persistence and obstinacy are what makes companies successful. The character is built during the third and fourth shots at attaining the goal. Not the first try. In trade, there are always myriads of things out of your control like the economy or your client's financial situations. But that's senseless reason to irritate and make kneejerk decisions. You just have to stay calm, cool and positive and try to keep moving. A great quote about persistence from Martin Luther King Jr. states that "If you can't fly you run if you can't run you walk if you can't walk you crawls. But no matter what, you keep moving forward."

Good plans are valueless without proper implementation. Plus flawless execution takes some practice. You can use up all the time in the world developing big plans for your business but if you do not brag the ability to perform on those plans you will surely fail. There also has to be buy-in across the board for organizations to be effectual at hitting their goals. Never discount the significance of having a proper plan and even better contingency strategies. But you need to keep in mind that if you spend proper time to make sure you have the capability to adapt as required, it won't feel like you are trying to steer a cruise ship when an iceberg placed in your pathway. It is perseverance that keeps you moving forward, having important goals are not achieved overnight, they necessitate, and no they demand patience, perseverance, and persistence. If you persistently take action, you will build momentum. "If Columbus had ever thought to turn back, no one would have blamed him. No one would have memorized him either."

In the face of challenge, perseverance ensures that we continue to take action towards the accomplishment of our

objective. As World's famous educationalist points out, this may require us to frequent adjustments to our tactics, until we achieve the objective.

"If you have an important point to make, don't try to be subtle or clever. Use a pile driver. Hit the point once. Then come back and hit it again. Then hit it a third time - a tremendous whack."— Winston S. Churchill

Reflecting on your objectives...

• Do you require amending the strategies you are using to archive your goal?

•   Have you persevered toward you objective? Or have you perhaps given up too soon?

There are two mentalities: buckle down and achieve your objectives, or not bother since you likely won't succeed in any case. In spite of the fact that this may appear to be an oversimplification, we think this oblivious choice has an aggravating impact all through your life. In the event that you are in the camp of "making a decent attempt leads to achievement", you invest more energy, you take rejection in your stride (despite the

fact that regardless it harms), you get up every single time you fall, and you feel motivated to attempt and attempt and try again until you succeed. Whether it's a spelling bee or beginning your own organization: trusting you can accomplish something through diligent work is a critical element for success. Be in the other camp of "you won't succeed" paying little heed to what you do, there is an unequivocally negative example. You feel that whatever you do throughout everyday life, you presumably won't succeed in any case, so you don't feel inspired to attempt in any case. When you confront difficulties and hurdles, you see that as a sign that you will fail. When you are rejected, again you feel weak, powerless and unfortunate.

In psychology, there's an idea called "locus of control": an individual's conviction about how long they can control the events around them: do you take control of the things you can control, or do you blame external components for your prosperity or disappointment. Sooner or later the vast majority have most likely identified with both camps. However, we imagine that over the time goes there is a huge exacerbating impact, encountering little hurdles and

difficulties and after that success, which inspires you to handle bigger challenges and to feel well prepared for greater misfortunes.

Set your psyche to an objective, something that you believe is bizarre and afterward buckles down to accomplish it. Depending upon the "challenge" you pick – it might take the number of hours or only a week. Learn a language, run more distant than you might suspect you could, and figure out how to cook another dish, get the courage to complete an open talking in Public, climb a mountain, build something, influence something, and create something. Set an objective that scares you a little and drives you out of your comfort zone. The truth is that you have accomplished something that you thought was unimaginable and not possible, you will be raring to go for your next toughest challenge and more resilient to the hindrances that you will unavoidably face out and along the way.

Here are 4 reasons Perseverance is vital to your prosperity and success:

1. PERSEVERANCE HELPS YOU CONQUER THE UNEXPECTED

At the point when things don't work out as expected, it's tempting to surrender. We lose

our confidence and consider moving onward to something that is less demanding. This is actually what the vast majorities of people do on the grounds that we're anxious about disappointment or failure and evade far from things that are hard and necessary. Plans make us feel safe, yet be prepared when things turn out of your control so you can land on your feet. You may need to change course and adjust somehow. Your objective continues to be the same as before, however, your roadmap may need to be changed. Try to develop a nimble mentality by attempting to anticipate potential misfortunes and have an alternate course of action for them.

2. PERSEVERANCE ENABLES YOU TO KEEP FOCUSED

At the point when things turn out badly, it is difficult to keep up motivation and core interest. Perseverance enables you to stay concentrated on long haul objectives so you can change your behavior accordingly. Regularly, this expects you to hold feelings in line to keep emotions in check from sabotaging your endeavors and efforts to continue advancing and moving forward. Visualize yourself achieving your objective regardless of what it takes. Watch out for

the objective and see yourself reaching the end.

3. PERSEVERANCE IS FED BY ENCOURAGEMENT AND SUPPORT

At the point when things turn out of your control, discover support and encouragement from people around you whom you trust and respect. In view of their experience and ability, search out their recommendation, suggestions, and proposals on the how to proficiently continue moving ahead. Successful individuals with perseverance comprehend that still need to do the tough work, yet it is extremely encouraging when you are surrounded with positive back up. Nobody is their very own island and we as a whole need other individuals' assistance and support. It may be a short talk or a couple of words of assistance. Be the individual who connects when you require assistance rather than to surrender. Do not be afraid to share your situations with other people, however, be particular about it. Ensure they are individuals who really need what is best for you and will give you both valuable and positive feedback. Seek for "mirror" companions or friends who will be fair, cherishing, honest, and objective.

4. PERSEVERANCE MAKES YOU DIG DEEP DOWN

If you are on a path that has meaning, value, and significance for you, you are unquestionably on the right path, so keep going. If you are not, then a delay or failure will be enough to make you surrender and try something else. Success can be exceptionally misleading on the grounds that frequently it is the place we remain, regardless of whether it's what truly fills us or not. It is a success that is based in complacency because we are too scared of failure to pursue the type of work that would offer worth and meaning. Don't take the easiest path, dig deep down where it counts and discovers the things that you can't leave; that are your true north. When you are pursuing that sort of objective, it won't make any difference what other individuals say on the grounds that your inner vision is far stronger than any external hindrance you will come up against.

Taking everything into account, in short, persistence is an essential piece of life. Its isolates the complete from the incomplete and just to recap, here are the 5 key reasons why having perseverance satisfies:

• Most successful persons have failed in any event once

- People jump at the chance to test you on the determination

- What comes effectively typically isn't justified, despite any potential benefits

- Knowledge isn't picked up without ingenuity and persistence

- The more you accomplish something, the better you get at it

Permanence, perseverance, and persistence in spite of all obstacles, discouragements, and impossibilities: It is this that in all things distinguishes the strong soul from the weak.

Why Persistence significant in our Life?

Persistence is the essences of accelerating your prospects of being successful in a specific thing or accomplishing a specific objective, and it likewise can assist you with staying motivated and continue striving towards the one long haul objective you want to achieve. For instance, when you first started your company, you most likely had dreams of success and recognition. You were positive that sales were reaching to pour in, and you'd be busy creating a great deal of cash. When you truly operated your company, it most likely dawned upon you rather quickly that hopes, visions, and

dreams alone weren't sufficient. Starting a business taught you that being a business owner isn't as simple as you once thought it might be. In fact, it's a great deal of labor with little reward gained at the outset. This is the reason why business failure rates are thus high. Folks merely cannot overcome the roadblocks and demands that accompany entrepreneurship.

The one word that may be used to describe businessperson who succeeds at business ownership is 'persistent'. You need to be persistent if you would like to be ready to sustain your business through the challenges and hurdles of entrepreneurship and sooner or later reap the rewards of a successful business. The truth is that Entrepreneurship comes with loads of ups and downs. Typically it feels as if you expertise a lot of downs than ups as you're within the early stages of business development. This is often once your mental attitude needs to stay optimistic and tough if you're getting to go through the hardships of constructing your business. If you're presently having a tough time in your business, you'd get advantage from reading some quotes regarding persistence. These quotes can assist you to understand that you simply

aren't the sole one who has undergone troubles as a business owner. Others are through what you're presently going through and possibly abundantly worse. But, they still built successful businesses despite their hurdles as a result of they remained to persevere.

The definition of Persistence is once you are desperate to do one thing considerably and not permitting anyone or any troubles stop you for doing it. This definition couldn't be any length suitable which is what the beauty of determination is and why it's therefore vital for anyone to have. With zero determination, it can lead you to give up on the single thing that you just needed to try to due to the issue that you just faced with or what somebody else has same. Nobody ought to ever surrender on one thing that they really need to try to as a result of everybody can achieve something if they are willing to place in the work a strong mindset towards overcoming the particular challenge and overcoming people that disagree and create trouble and don't have your best interest to your life.

Why Persistence is significant than planning?

We are mysterious creatures. Anguish and hope can coexist and still create something astonishing. Perseverance is the ability to maintain action despite your feelings. It has a lot to do with your life's success and business success. It is considered as an omnipotent. An American politician Calvin Coolidge once stated "The slogan "press on" has solved and always will solve the troubles of the human race". Intelligence and ability cannot take the place of persistence. The worth of persistence comes from a visualization of the future that is so compelling you would give approx anything to make it factual or real. Persistence of action draws closer from the persistence of vision. When you are specifically clear about what you want in such a way that your vision does not change much, you will be more unfailing and persistentin your dealings. Hence, that consistency of action will produce consistency of outcomes. One favorite quote state that "no plan survives first contact with the enemy." We have learned this reality time and time again. Mike Tyson put it well when he stated, "Everybody has an arrangement until the

point when they get punched in the face." Regular arranging is basic to maintain a business yet we find that readiness and steadiness are significantly more imperative that the most ideal marketable strategy. Clear emergency courses of action were basic for mission achievement.

Here are reasons that being well-prepared and persistent to tackle life's obstruction is significant than trying to manage things out of your control.

Things do not generally go as planned, thus be ready when the inevitable obstruction or hurdles stand in your way. Whether you are the team member of the big-giant corporation or an entrepreneur growing a start-up, you have probably noticed that plans can change, and change often. But the enterprise has to be well-structured to remain dynamic, robust and strong. Good leaders must continue focused on what lays ahead for foreseeing potential blockage and adjust accordingly. Experiencing letdown along your path to accomplishment does not mean you failed. Failure generally occurs when you allow those experiences cause you to give up. Planning does not ensure

adaptableness. In the Teams, while doing fight dive training we had a saying, "Plan your dive, & dive your plan." Things can get confusing underwater in pitch blackness, however, when you start second guess yourself, it can snowball uncontrollable. That's why it is said, good old fashion common sense is also a great reserve and stand-in when your plan starts falling apart.

For companies, o be adapt and dynamic to external and internal forces pushing against them, they must have robust financials, nimble leadership, and a team with a shared sense of purpose. Planning does not identify unknowns. Persistence and obstinacy are what makes companies successful. The character is built during the third and fourth shots at attaining the goal. Not the first try. In trade, there are always myriads of things out of your control like the economy or your client's financial situations. But that's senseless reason to irritate and make kneejerk decisions. You just have to stay calm, cool and positive and try to keep moving. A great quote about persistence from Martin Luther King Jr. states that "If you can't fly you run if you can't run you walk if you can't walk you crawls. But no matter what, you keep moving forward."

Good plans are valueless without proper implementation. Plus flawless execution takes some practice. You can use up all the time in the world developing big plans for your business but if you do not brag the ability to perform on those plans you will surely fail. There also has to be buy-in across the board for organizations to be effectual at hitting their goals. Never discount the significance of having a proper plan and even better contingency strategies. But you need to keep in mind that if you spend proper time to make sure you have the capability to adapt as required, it won't feel like you are trying to steer a cruise ship when an iceberg placed in your pathway. It is perseverance that keeps you moving forward, having important goals are not achieved overnight, they necessitate, and no they demand patience, perseverance, and persistence. If you persistently take action, you will build momentum. "If Columbus had ever thought to turn back, no one would have blamed him. No one would have memorized him either."

In the face of challenge, perseverance ensures that we continue to take action towards the accomplishment of our

objective. As World's famous educationalist points out, this may require us to frequent adjustments to our tactics, until we achieve the objective.

"If you have an important point to make, don't try to be subtle or clever. Use a pile driver. Hit the point once. Then come back and hit it again. Then hit it a third time - a tremendous whack."— Winston S. Churchill

Reflecting on your objectives...

• Do you require amending the strategies you are using to archive your goal?

• Have you persevered toward you objective? Or have you perhaps given up too soon?

There are two mentalities: buckle down and achieve your objectives, or not bother since you likely won't succeed in any case. In spite of the fact that this may appear to be an oversimplification, we think this oblivious choice has an aggravating impact all through your life. In the event that you are in the camp of "making a decent attempt leads to achievement", you invest more energy, you take rejection in your stride (despite the

fact that regardless it harms), you get up every single time you fall, and you feel motivated to attempt and attempt and try again until you succeed. Whether it's a spelling bee or beginning your own organization: trusting you can accomplish something through diligent work is a critical element for success. Be in the other camp of "you won't succeed" paying little heed to what you do, there is an unequivocally negative example. You feel that whatever you do throughout everyday life, you presumably won't succeed in any case, so you don't feel inspired to attempt in any case. When you confront difficulties and hurdles, you see that as a sign that you will fail. When you are rejected, again you feel weak, powerless and unfortunate.

In psychology, there's an idea called "locus of control": an individual's conviction about how long they can control the events around them: do you take control of the things you can control, or do you blame external components for your prosperity or disappointment. Sooner or later the vast majority have most likely identified with both camps. However, we imagine that over the time goes there is a huge exacerbating impact, encountering little hurdles and

difficulties and after that success, which inspires you to handle bigger challenges and to feel well prepared for greater misfortunes.

Set your psyche to an objective, something that you believe is bizarre and afterward buckles down to accomplish it. Depending upon the "challenge" you pick – it might take the number of hours or only a week. Learn a language, run more distant than you might suspect you could, and figure out how to cook another dish, get the courage to complete an open talking in Public, climb a mountain, build something, influence something, and create something. Set an objective that scares you a little and drives you out of your comfort zone. The truth is that you have accomplished something that you thought was unimaginable and not possible, you will be raring to go for your next toughest challenge and more resilient to the hindrances that you will unavoidably face out and along the way.

Here are 4 reasons Perseverance is vital to your prosperity and success:

CHAPTER5. PERSEVERANCE HELPS YOU CONQUER THE UNEXPECTED

At the point when things don't work out as expected, it's tempting to surrender. We lose

our confidence and consider moving onward to something that is less demanding. This is actually what the vast majorities of people do on the grounds that we're anxious about disappointment or failure and evade far from things that are hard and necessary. Plans make us feel safe, yet be prepared when things turn out of your control so you can land on your feet. You may need to change course and adjust somehow. Your objective continues to be the same as before, however, your roadmap may need to be changed. Try to develop a nimble mentality by attempting to anticipate potential misfortunes and have an alternate course of action for them.

2. PERSEVERANCE ENABLES YOU TO KEEP FOCUSED

At the point when things turn out badly, it is difficult to keep up motivation and core interest. Perseverance enables you to stay concentrated on long haul objectives so you can change your behavior accordingly. Regularly, this expects you to hold feelings in line to keep emotions in check from sabotaging your endeavors and efforts to continue advancing and moving forward. Visualize yourself achieving your objective regardless of what it takes. Watch out for

the objective and see yourself reaching the end.

3. PERSEVERANCE IS FED BY ENCOURAGEMENT AND SUPPORT

At the point when things turn out of your control, discover support and encouragement from people around you whom you trust and respect. In view of their experience and ability, search out their recommendation, suggestions, and proposals on the how to proficiently continue moving ahead. Successful individuals with perseverance comprehend that still need to do the tough work, yet it is extremely encouraging when you are surrounded with positive back up. Nobody is their very own island and we as a whole need other individuals' assistance and support. It may be a short talk or a couple of words of assistance. Be the individual who connects when you require assistance rather than to surrender. Do not be afraid to share your situations with other people, however, be particular about it. Ensure they are individuals who really need what is best for you and will give you both valuable and positive feedback. Seek for "mirror" companions or friends who will be fair, cherishing, honest, and objective.

4. PERSEVERANCE MAKES YOU DIG DEEP DOWN

If you are on a path that has meaning, value, and significance for you, you are unquestionably on the right path, so keep going. If you are not, then a delay or failure will be enough to make you surrender and try something else. Success can be exceptionally misleading on the grounds that frequently it is the place we remain, regardless of whether it's what truly fills us or not. It is a success that is based in complacency because we are too scared of failure to pursue the type of work that would offer worth and meaning. Don't take the easiest path, dig deep down where it counts and discovers the things that you can't leave; that are your true north. When you are pursuing that sort of objective, it won't make any difference what other individuals say on the grounds that your inner vision is far stronger than any external hindrance you will come up against.

Taking everything into account, in short, persistence is an essential piece of life. Its isolates the complete from the incomplete and just to recap, here are the 5 key reasons why having perseverance satisfies:

• Most successful persons have failed in any event once

• People jump at the chance to test you on the determination

• What comes effectively typically isn't justified, despite any potential benefits

• Knowledge isn't picked up without ingenuity and persistence

• The more you accomplish something, the better you get at it

Permanence, perseverance, and persistence in spite of all obstacles, discouragements, and impossibilities: It is this that in all things distinguishes the strong soul from the weak.

Why Persistence significant in our Life?

Persistence is the essences of accelerating your prospects of being successful in a specific thing or accomplishing a specific objective, and it likewise can assist you with staying motivated and continue striving towards the one long haul objective you want to achieve. For instance, when you first started your company, you most likely had dreams of success and recognition. You were positive that sales were reaching to pour in, and you'd be busy creating a great deal of cash. When you truly operated your company, it most likely dawned upon you rather quickly that hopes, visions, and

dreams alone weren't sufficient. Starting a business taught you that being a business owner isn't as simple as you once thought it might be. In fact, it's a great deal of labor with little reward gained at the outset. This is the reason why business failure rates are thus high. Folks merely cannot overcome the roadblocks and demands that accompany entrepreneurship.

The one word that may be used to describe businessperson who succeeds at business ownership is 'persistent'. You need to be persistent if you would like to be ready to sustain your business through the challenges and hurdles of entrepreneurship and sooner or later reap the rewards of a successful business. The truth is that Entrepreneurship comes with loads of ups and downs. Typically it feels as if you expertise a lot of downs than ups as you're within the early stages of business development. This is often once your mental attitude needs to stay optimistic and tough if you're getting to go through the hardships of constructing your business. If you're presently having a tough time in your business, you'd get advantage from reading some quotes regarding persistence. These quotes can assist you to understand that you simply

aren't the sole one who has undergone troubles as a business owner. Others are through what you're presently going through and possibly abundantly worse. But, they still built successful businesses despite their hurdles as a result of they remained to persevere.

The definition of Persistence is once you are desperate to do one thing considerably and not permitting anyone or any troubles stop you for doing it. This definition couldn't be any length suitable which is what the beauty of determination is and why it's therefore vital for anyone to have. With zero determination, it can lead you to give up on the single thing that you just needed to try to due to the issue that you just faced with or what somebody else has same. Nobody ought to ever surrender on one thing that they really need to try to as a result of everybody can achieve something if they are willing to place in the work a strong mindset towards overcoming the particular challenge and overcoming people that disagree and create trouble and don't have your best interest to your life.

Why Persistence is significant than planning?

We are mysterious creatures. Anguish and hope can coexist and still create something astonishing. Perseverance is the ability to maintain action despite your feelings. It has a lot to do with your life's success and business success. It is considered as an omnipotent. An American politician Calvin Coolidge once stated "The slogan "press on" has solved and always will solve the troubles of the human race". Intelligence and ability cannot take the place of persistence. The worth of persistence comes from a visualization of the future that is so compelling you would give approx anything to make it factual or real. Persistence of action draws closer from the persistence of vision. When you are specifically clear about what you want in such a way that your vision does not change much, you will be more unfailing and persistent inyour dealings. Hence, that consistency of action will produce consistency of outcomes. One favorite quote state that "no plan survives first contact with the enemy." We have learned this reality time and time again. Mike Tyson put it well when he stated, "Everybody has an arrangement until the point when they get punched in the face." Regular reviewing isone of best practices for maintaining a profitable business yet we find that readiness and steadiness are significantly more imperative that the most ideal marketable strategy. Clear emergency courses of action were basic for mission achievement.

Here are reasons that being well-prepared and persistent to tackle life's obstruction is significant than trying to manage things out of your control.

Things do not generally go as planned, thus be ready when the inevitable obstruction or hurdles stand in your way. Whether you are the team member of the big-giant corporation or an entrepreneur growing a start-up, you have probably noticed that plans can change, and change often. But the enterprise has to be well-structured to remain dynamic, robust and strong. Good leaders must continue focused on what lays ahead for foreseeing potential blockage and adjust accordingly. Experiencing letdown along your path to accomplishment does not mean you failed. Failure generally occurs when you allow those experiences cause you to give up. Planning does not ensure adaptableness. In the Teams, while doing fight dive training we had a saying, "Plan your dive, & dive your plan." Things can get confusing underwater in pitch blackness, however, when you start second guess yourself, it can snowball uncontrollable. That's why it is said, good old fashion common sense is also a great reserve and stand-in when your plan starts falling apart.

For companies, o be adapt and dynamic to external and internal forces pushing against them, they must have robust financials, nimble leadership, and a team with a shared sense of purpose. Planning does not identify unknowns. Persistence and obstinacy are what makes companies successful. The character is built during the third and fourth shots at attaining the goal. Not the first try. In trade, there are always myriads of things out of your control like the economy or your client's financial situations. But that's senseless reason to irritate and make kneejerk decisions. You just have to stay calm, cool and positive and try to keep moving. A great quote about persistence from Martin Luther King Jr. states that "If you can't fly you run if you can't run you walk if you can't walk you crawls. But no matter what, you keep moving forward."

Good plans are valueless without proper implementation. Plus flawless execution takes some practice. You can use up all the time in the world developing big plans for your business but if you do not brag the ability to perform on those plans you will surely fail. There also has to be buy-in across the board for organizations to be effectual at hitting their goals. Never discount the significance of having a proper plan and even better contingency strategies. But you need to keep in mind that if you spend proper time to make sure you have the capability to adapt as required, it won't feel like you are trying to steer a cruise ship when an iceberg placed in your pathway. It is perseverance that keeps you moving forward, having important goals are not achieved overnight, they necessitate, and no they demand patience, perseverance, and persistence. If you persistently take action, you will build momentum. "If Columbus had ever thought to turn back, no one would have blamed him. No one would have memorized him either."

In the face of challenge, perseverance ensures that we continue to take action towards the accomplishment of our objective. As World's famous educationalist points out, this may require us to frequent adjustments to our tactics, until we achieve the objective.

"If you have an important point to make, don't try to be subtle or clever. Use a pile driver. Hit the point once. Then come back and hit it again. Then hit it a third time - a tremendous whack."— Winston S. Churchill

Reflecting on your objectives...

• Do you require amending the strategies you are using to archive your goal?

• Have you persevered toward you objective? Or have you perhaps given up too soon?

There are two mentalities: buckle down and achieve your objectives, or not bother since you likely won't succeed in any case. In spite of the fact that this may appear to be an oversimplification, we think this oblivious choice has an aggravating impact all through your life. In the event that you are in the camp of "making a decent attempt leads to achievement", you invest more energy, you take rejection in your stride (despite the fact that regardless it harms), you get up every single time you fall, and you feel motivated to attempt and attempt and try again until you succeed. Whether it's a spelling bee or beginning your own organization: trusting you can accomplish something through diligent work is a critical element for success. Be in the other camp of "you won't succeed" paying little heed to what you do, there is an unequivocally negative example. You feel that whatever you do throughout everyday life, you presumably won't succeed in any case, so you don't feel inspired to attempt in any case. When you confront difficulties and hurdles, you see that as a sign that you will fail. When you are rejected, again you feel weak, powerless and unfortunate.

In psychology, there's an idea called "locus of control": an individual's conviction about how long they can control the events around them: do you take control of the things you can control, or do you blame external components for your prosperity or disappointment. Sooner or later the vast majority have most likely identified with both camps. However, we imagine that over the time goes there is a huge exacerbating impact, encountering little hurdles and difficulties and after that success, which inspires you to handle bigger challenges and to feel well prepared for greater misfortunes.

Set your psyche to an objective, something that you believe is bizarre and afterward buckles down to accomplish it. Depending upon the "challenge" you pick – it might take the number of hours or only a week. Learn a language, run more distant than you might suspect you could, and figure out how to cook another dish, get the courage to complete an open talking in Public, climb a mountain, build something, influence something, and create something. Set an objective that scares you a little and drives you out of your comfort zone. The truth is that you have accomplished something that you thought was unimaginable and not possible, you will be raring to go for your next toughest challenge and more resilient to the hindrances that you will unavoidably face out and along the way.

Here are 4 reasons Perseverance is vital to your prosperity and success:

1. PERSEVERANCE HELPS YOU CONQUER THE UNEXPECTED

At the point when things don't work out as expected, it's tempting to surrender. We lose our confidence and consider moving onward to something that is less demanding. This is actually what the vast majorities of people do on the grounds that we're anxious about disappointment or failure and evade far from things that are hard and necessary. Plans make us feel safe, yet be prepared when things turn out of your control so you can land on your feet. You may need to change course and adjust somehow. Your objective continues to be the same as before, however, your roadmap may need to be changed. Try to develop a nimble mentality by attempting to anticipate potential misfortunes and have an alternate course of action for them.

2. PERSEVERANCE ENABLES YOU TO KEEP FOCUSED

At the point when things turn out badly, it is difficult to keep up motivation and core interest. Perseverance enables you to stay concentrated on long haul objectives so you can change your behavior accordingly. Regularly, this expects you to hold feelings in line to keep emotions in check from sabotaging your endeavors and efforts to continue advancing and moving forward. Visualize yourself achieving your objective regardless of what it takes. Watch out for the objective and see yourself reaching the end.

3. PERSEVERANCE IS FED BY ENCOURAGEMENT AND SUPPORT

At the point when things turn out of your control, discover support and encouragement from people around you whom you trust and respect. In view of their experience and ability, search out their recommendation, suggestions, and proposals on the how to proficiently continue moving ahead. Successful individuals with perseverance comprehend that still need to do the tough work, yet it is extremely encouraging when you are surrounded with positive back up. Nobody is their very own island and we as a whole need other individuals' assistance and support. It may be a short talk or a couple of words of assistance. Be the individual who connects when you require assistance rather than to surrender. Do not be afraid to share your situations with other people, however, be particular about it. Ensure they are individuals who really need what is best for you and will give you both valuable and positive feedback. Seek for "mirror" companions or friends who will be fair, cherishing, honest, and objective.

4. PERSEVERANCE MAKES YOU DIG DEEP DOWN

If you are on a path that has meaning, value, and significance for you, you are unquestionably on the right path, so keep going. If you are not, then a delay or failure will be enough to make you surrender and try something else. Success can be exceptionally misleading on the grounds that frequently it is the place we remain, regardless of whether it's what truly fills us or not. It is a success that is based in complacency because we are too scared of failure to pursue the type of work that would offer worth and meaning. Don't take the easiest path, dig deep down where it counts and discovers the things that you can't leave; that are your true north. When you are pursuing that sort of objective, it won't make any difference what other individuals say on the grounds that your inner vision is far stronger than any external hindrance you will come up against.

Taking everything into account, in short, persistence is an essential piece of life. Its isolates the complete from the incomplete and just to recap, here are the 5 key reasons why having perseverance satisfies:

• Most successful persons have failed in any event once

• People jump at the chance to test you on the determination

• What comes effectively typically isn't justified, despite any potential benefits

• Knowledge isn't picked up without ingenuity and persistence

• The more you accomplish something, the better you get at it

Permanence, perseverance, and persistence in spite of all obstacles, discouragements, and impossibilities: It is this that in all things distinguishes the strong soul from the weak.

ABOUT THE AUTHOR

Positive Thinking Mentor Author Gautam Sharma(gautamsharma.contact@gmail.com)-an intelligent, accomplished, capable, creative professional was born in India, has lived in Asia, Europe, Africa and now living in USA embodies and edifies positive thinking, power of optimism and is sharing insights into human behavior and human potential through philosophical, psychological perspectives with the view of sharing mankind's centuries-old wisdom plus proven, research findings so as to empower people worldwide. The author plans to utilize his strengths of professionalism, wide, varied experiences, creativity and communications' skills to publish the Empowerment Series on improvement, self-help topics. Thank you valued readers for your continuous support, contributions and your favorable feedback. Wishing everybody abundance of positive thinking and better living through the power of optimism.

OTHER BOOKS BY THE AUTHOR

https://www.amazon.com/POSITIVE-THINKING-OPTIMISM-Original-English-ebook/dp/B01HRY684S/ref=asap_bc?ie=UTF8

also

 https://www.amazon.com/SELF-CONFIDENCE-ESTEEM-HAPPINESS-SUCCESS-ebook/dp/B076VM1MNR/ref=tmm_kin_swatch_0?_encoding=UTF8&qid=&sr=

 and

https://www.amazon.com/JOY-forHEALTHY-HAPPY-LIVING-Empowerment-ebook/dp/B078L6Y1YM/ref=sr_1_5?s=digital-text&ie=UTF8&qid=1515281796&sr=1-5

Discover your full potential: The Universe within

Gautam Sharma

 (Dedicated to valued readers, especially those who write positive reviews)

www.ingramcontent.com/pod-product-compliance
Lightning Source LLC
Chambersburg PA
CBHW061806250726

48657CB00001B/304